LEGAL EDUCATION IN THE WESTERN WORLD

LEGAL EDUCATION IN THE WESTERN WORLD

A Cultural and Comparative History

Rogelio Pérez-Perdomo

Translated by Anapaula Pérez and Rosa Meléndez

STANFORD UNIVERSITY PRESS
Stanford, California

Stanford University Press
Stanford, California

Printed in the United States of America on acid-free, archival-quality paper

Library of Congress Cataloging-in-Publication Data

Names: Pérez-Perdomo, Rogelio, author.
Title: Legal education in the Western world : a cultural and comparative history / Rogelio Pérez-Perdomo.
Other titles: Educacioìn juriìdica en Occidente. English
Description: Stanford, California : Stanford University Press, 2024. | Translation of: Educacioìn juriìdica en Occidente : una historia cultural / Rogelio Pérez-Perdomo. Valencia : Tirant Humanidades, 2022. | Includes bibliographical references and index.
Identifiers: LCCN 2023057999 (print) | LCCN 2023058000 (ebook) | ISBN 9781503637207 (cloth) | ISBN 9781503639041 (paperback) | ISBN 9781503639058 (epub)
Subjects: LCSH: Law—Study and teaching—America—History. | Law—Study and teaching—Europe—History.
Classification: LCC K100 .P4713 2024 (print) | LCC K100 (ebook) | DDC 340.071/01821—dc23/eng/20240117
LC record available at https://lccn.loc.gov/2023057999
LC ebook record available at https://lccn.loc.gov/2023058000

Cover design: Michele Wetherbee
Cover photography: Shutterstock
Typeset by Newgen in Baskerville URW 10/14

For Isabella and Thomas

CONTENTS

ACKNOWLEDGMENTS

I feel that I have been developing this work throughout my entire academic life. My concern with and study of different ways of approaching the educational task in law began practically from my first days as a professor. My first book, published many years ago, was on methods of legal education (Pérez Perdomo, 1974). For this reason, I owe thanks to many institutions and people. In particular, I want to mention the Universidad Central de Venezuela, where I studied law and developed my career as a professor-researcher at a time when the university could support study and research trips to various countries. In Paris, Michel Villey and René David helped me define my vocation. At Harvard, Lon Fuller, Roberto Unger, and John Dawson guided me in different approaches to law. At Perugia, Alessandro Giuliani pointed me to the field of legal education as a great research topic and invited me to write about it. As a professor at the Instituto de Estudios Superiores de Administración (IESA) in Caracas, I was able to approach the teaching of the law in a business school and to explore its relationship with economics and ethics. The International Institute of Sociology of Law of Oñati allowed me to get to know an amazing institution that is basically a network of scholars. It offered me the opportunity to discuss the topic of comparative legal education with master's-degree students from various countries around the world. At the Universidad Metropolitana de Caracas, I had the opportunity to create a law school and to experience legal education from a dean's perspective, as well as to teach law for many years. Over the past twenty years, Stanford Law School has allowed me to coteach with two admirable professors, John Henry Merryman and Lawrence M. Friedman, to interact with a group of remarkable professors and students, and to enjoy an extraordinary library. I should also mention shorter stays at universities in Chile, Colombia, Mexico, Peru, the Max Planck Institut für Europäische Rechtgeschichte, and Florida International University.

In writing this book, I am especially grateful for the comments and suggestions on early drafts of Amalia Kessler, Manuel Gómez, Luis Bergolla, and Edmundo Fuenzalida. The assistance of Sergio Stone and the staff of the Stanford Law School library was invaluable in consulting the bibliography that has supported this effort. I thank the Centro de Estudios sobre la Enseñanza y el Aprendizaje del Derecho (CEEAD) in Mexico City and the Instituto de Historia del Derecho in Buenos Aires for organizing discussions of the Spanish version of the work in which I received very useful comments. Finally, I must thank the two anonymous readers at Stanford University Press who gave me comments that facilitated a revision that makes the English version perhaps less flawed than the Spanish version, as well as Marcela Maxfield and others at Stanford University Press for their support in editing this version. Anapaula Pérez and Rosa Meléndez translated the Spanish version into English. Sonne Lemke checked the translation, carefully reviewed and edited the manuscript and proofs, and caught many of my mistakes. I am deeply indebted to all these wonderful people. The mistakes that remain are entirely my responsibility.

LEGAL EDUCATION IN THE WESTERN WORLD

Introduction

Legal education is often seen as a minor field of study. The term broadly refers to understanding how young people can be prepared to work in legal professions, how ideas about the law are transmitted, and how young people come to know the language, fundamental legal concepts, and terminology used in the discipline of law. This book argues that the study of legal education is much larger than just pedagogy. Legal education is linked to the law as a way of ordering society and to the conceptualization of the law itself. It is also related to the place that the key actors in the legal system occupy in the polity and society. By offering a history and analysis of legal education through its most general features, we can dive into the history of the legal discipline, the structure of regulations, and the profession of those who have to deal with those regulations. The work explores the relationship of the ideas or notions of the law, legal knowledge, and the social role of the most important legal actors, those who today we call legal professionals but who have had other titles historically.

This work has a historical dimension, but it does not pretend to be a chronological or exhaustive history of legal education. Instead, what it proposes is an exploration of the relationship between legal education and its social and intellectual context in selected periods and cultures. In that sense, this work is intended as an introduction to a cultural and comparative history of the law. It is a *longue durée* history with a temporal scope of two millennia. Within that broad scope, certain periods and places have been selected in which the relationships of legal education, the concept of the law, and the social role of the main legal actors can be clearly highlighted and in which the fundamental changes in these aspects of the law can be easily discerned. The geographical framework chosen for this work is Europe and the Americas. The distinction between chapters is taken from the *summa divisio* of comparative law between the civil law and common law traditions, except for the final chapter, which analyzes the contact between and convergence of the two traditions in contemporary times.

This book is about the changes in the legal education of both civil and common law traditions. A legal tradition is the most settled part of the legal culture in relation to understanding the law and how we relate to it (Merryman & Pérez-Perdomo, 2019:2). It generally corresponds to the basic aspects of the way those who are most closely associated with the law understand it; this is what we call the professional culture of law. "Tradition" in itself implies continuity in time but does not exclude changes. The purpose of this work, then, is to show the changes that legal education has undergone in these two great traditions of the Western world.

At the same time, legal education helps maintain legal tradition. It is charged with transmitting the currently accepted ideas and values related to the law, as well as the law's proper relationship with society. For this reason, studying legal education historically and analyzing it from the perspective of the establishment and transmission of legal culture can offer a new window onto legal culture. Thus, this work is a cultural history of the law, or at least part of that history. It is a contribution to thinking about legal education both historically and theoretically, a perspective that has been rarely offered (Dezalay & Garth, 2021), even among those of us who are professionally dedicated to the teaching of law (Cownie, 1999).

Legal education is also important in relation to those whom we now call legal professionals. What really distinguishes them from other mortals is having received a special education that others have not received and being directly or indirectly linked to the operation of the legal system. Of course, it is important to distinguish formal from informal learning.

The latter is more difficult to delineate because it is intermingled with many other influences, such as the general education of certain social strata and the very activity of legal professionals or experts. This book focuses on formal education. Nevertheless, it offers some glimpses of the informal aspect of legal education. The analysis relies on what we know about the Roman jurisconsults, the medieval law professors and lawyers, the humanist jurists of the early modern age, and the professors and lawyers of later centuries, all in relation to their place and roles in society.

As a work of cultural history, this book is supported by an extensive bibliography, generally classified as works on the history of law, the philosophy of law, or the history of legal ideas, but the emphasis of the analysis is sociocultural. Preference has been given to documents from the period, such as the testimonies of professors, students, and visitors. Consideration has also been given to the literature used by students or trainees, mainly in order to understand the structure and type of discourse as a reflection of the general concept of the law rather than to analyze the ideas in detail. For the most recent decades, I also incorporate some self-study, drawing from my experience as a student and teacher in several countries in Europe and the Americas, with the goal of contrasting the observations derived from my own experience with the conclusions of academic works.

The first chapter deals with the civil law tradition starting with the transformations during the long period from classical Rome to the time of Justinian. It then moves to the development of law teaching in medieval universities and the subsequent changes that occurred in Europe and Latin America. The chapter focuses on the main transformations in a tradition that extends from the first century BC to the beginning of the twentieth century but highlights those times and places in which one can perceive most clearly the relationships between legal education and other relevant aspects of the law.

The second chapter analyzes the common law tradition. The story begins in England, where the education of serjeants-at-law and barristers can be traced from the end of the Middle Ages to the beginning of the twentieth century. The focus then shifts to the transformations of legal education in the United States of America, especially from the nineteenth century onward.

The third chapter analyzes the convergence that has occurred in Europe and in the Americas as the result of a new conception of the law, legal knowledge, and the role of legal professionals in a time of very rapid social change and frequent interactions among people from different nations and cultures.

I

The Civil Law Tradition

EUROPE AND LATIN AMERICA

Latin American and European legal communities recognize that their conception of the law and many of their rules are rooted in ancient Rome. The continuing and widespread interest in those origins is evident in the fact that many Latin American and European universities still include Roman law as a mandatory subject. In English, the universal designation of this tradition has been "civil law," for the key role that the *Corpus Iuris Civilis,* a compilation of Roman law, has had in the teaching of law from the twelfth to the eighteenth century (Glendon, Carozza, & Picker, 2008; Merryman & Pérez-Perdomo, 2019). In the languages of the civil law countries, the designation of their own tradition is not consistent. In Spanish, the term "Roman-canonical" is commonly used, and it reflects the role of canon law, or the law of the Catholic Church, in the teaching and configuration of law from medieval times onward. René David (1964), the leading French comparative law scholar, uses the term "Romano-Germanic family." In other texts it has been simply referred to as "Roman" or even "continental law," in recognition of its expansion throughout the European continent.

At the outset of this survey, it is important to recognize that Greek philosophers made essential contribution to Roman law by developing a theory of justice and conceiving of methodologies for analyzing social phenomena (e.g., prudence, dialectic). These methodologies facilitated the organization of Roman law and transformed it into a form of knowledge that could be reliably transmitted. Both ancient Greeks and ancient Romans defined the law as that which is just, but the definition of the field as something distinct from religion, social norms, or ethics was entirely a product of the ancient Romans. Schiavone (2009) calls this development the invention of law in the West. Other civilizations have had rules of conduct that we now consider part of the law, but they were closely linked to religion, such as Sharia in the case of the Islamic tradition (Abdulla & Keshavjee, 2018), or to social norms (as the *li*) or to the exercise of power (like the *fa*), both rooted in Chinese tradition (Li, 1999). Later, analysis will show that religion, social norms, and political power have had an important influence on the legal field, notwithstanding the fact that Western law has been thought of as independent of these mechanisms of social ordering.

It was in Rome that the law effectively originated as a specific field of knowledge and human action. Furthermore, ancient Romans developed an education system for training individuals in the field. These developments have had an enormous impact over the ensuing centuries, as reflected in the fact that Roman law constituted the core of legal studies until the eighteenth century, although the exact conception of Roman law varied according to the epoch. For example, Christianity transformed the conception of humankind and the world and thus substantially influenced politics, education, and the law. In the twelfth century, the law of the Catholic Church, known as canon law, was added to legal studies. But despite the introduction of these novel ideas, Roman law was still recognized as the origin of the fundamental concepts and ideas of the law.

In the nineteenth century, social and political changes stimulated another substantial transformation of law and legal education. Two monumental creations, national constitutions and legal codes, changed the legal field and legal education. The law became national, and its content and educational methods changed. Constitutional, commercial, criminal, procedural, family, and other branches of national law were added to the curriculum. International law became a new subject as well. At a deeper level, the very concept of the law varied significantly, and—I would argue—these changes influenced the way the law was taught. This is the object of analysis in this chapter.

The chapter is divided into three sections that explore the relations between legal education and the conception of the law at selected moments in history. The guiding hypothesis is that the way the law is taught and studied, as well as the content that is being taught, depends on how the law is conceived and on its development within a social and historical context. These dimensions are in turn related to the thinking of those individuals who are considered law experts or who are in charge of transmitting this knowledge. The main purpose here is to explore the content, methods, and institutions of legal education and their relation to the idea of the law as a whole, and also to examine the role of those who teach or practice the law. The first section is dedicated to the transformations of those issues in ancient Rome, including the work of Justinian. The second section constitutes an analysis of late medieval and modern Europe. In the third and final sections, the analysis focuses on these issues in Latin America, particularly since the codification of the law. These periods basically correspond with those identified by Lessafer (2009). The concluding section discusses the tension between continuity and change in this long tradition. The recent past, from the second half of the twentieth century to the present, is covered in the third chapter of the book.

LEGAL EDUCATION FROM CLASSIC ROME TO JUSTINIAN

Ancient Roman law itself has a long history, from about 750 BC to Justinian (emperor, AD 527–565). The initial period of ancient Roman law is known as archaic, and it concludes with the Twelve Tables (453 BC), the oldest important document of Roman law. The subsequent period is called the praetorian or honorary period. During these first periods, documents were scarce because oral culture was predominant. We therefore know little about the law or legal education in these times. The classic period is generally considered the most significant for the development of law. The central personages were the jurisconsults who wrote extensively about law. During this period, legal knowledge was organized, the first schools were established, and the first textbooks were written. After the classic period, the emperors' contributions grew in significance. Justinian oversaw a compilation of legal knowledge that became very important for medieval and early modern law and legal education.

In the early history of Roman law, the praetors are considered to have generated a phase of creativity and intense development. At that time, Rome was a city organized around clans or family groups that consisted of everyone under the authority of the paterfamilias, or head of the family clan, regardless of their blood ties. The law was designed to regulate the relationships of the patresfamilias. Not every complaint could be brought before the public authorities, which is why it was so important to define the ones that could be. For this purpose, the senate designated praetors, who acted as magistrates for a one-year term. At the beginning of his term, the praetor published the actions that would be recognized as justiciable. This was called the praetor's edict (*edictum praetoris*). The first praetor (later titled the urban praetor) was named in 366 BC. When the population of Rome started to grow and the presence of foreigners (*peregrini*) became more conspicuous, the senate created a second praetorship in 242 BC that dealt with the conflicts between foreigners and also between foreigners and Roman citizens. This figure was known as the *praetor peregrinus*.

The praetor was not a judge. His role was to formulate a short description of the nature of the conflict being presented (the written *formula*). Then, a person was chosen as the *iudex* to decide the case. The praetor's formulation outlined the case, and the *iudex* was limited to considering only the points that the praetor had enunciated. It should be noted that in terms of modern law, the *iudex* had a role closer to that of an arbiter or mediator than to a judge. This system for limiting the types of conflicts to be adjudicated paved the way for the development of law because it focused on acts with consequences that needed to be analyzed thoroughly and independently of the people who carried them out. It is also important to point out that there was no apparatus or system for executing the decisions of the *iudex*, but we can assume that social norms effectively ensured voluntary compliance, given that this system helped to maintain peace and order between the families that constituted the social fabric of Rome.

The legal field gradually acquired shape as the praetors began distinguishing the actions that were justiciable from those that were not. Thus, for example, only the relationships between the patresfamilias were actionable; relationships within the family were not a concern of the law. Certain types of conduct were gradually included (or excluded) as the domain of the law took shape. Nonetheless, the resulting knowledge remained diffuse and casuist, so it could not be properly taught or studied.

The praetor and the *iudex* were not necessarily considered expert in law. They were therefore frequently advised by elders with more experience and knowledge who contributed their *auctoritas* to the decision-making. *Auctoritas* was associated with the moral and intellectual prestige of a person. These individuals with *auctoritas* did not have any specific accreditation, but their opinions were taken into account because of their high social standing and the esteem they enjoyed within Roman society because of their *dignitas* (García Pelayo, 1969). These individuals gradually achieved special recognition as jurisconsults. By the end of the first century BC, the emperor Augustus gave political recognition to a group of them, the *ius publicum respondendi*. Subsequent emperors continued this practice. What that recognition meant has been a frequent topic of discussion, but it did not make the jurisconsults public officers, nor did it give them the exclusive privilege of providing consultations to the praetors or judges. Other respected individuals could be consulted as well (Paricio, 2018).

The documents of that period identify individuals who were considered jurisconsults, or at least the most prominent ones. We also know that there were several people who performed similar duties even before the classic period. Nevertheless, what differentiates the jurisconsults and makes them stand out in the history of law is the fact that they wrote about the rules and organized the opinions that they and others had provided. In that sense, they recorded and gave structure to the legal knowledge that had been developing over the course of three centuries. The legal rules were formulated in *lege* (approved proposals in the comitia, or hierarchical organized public meetings), *plebiscita*, *edicta praetorius*, and *senatus consulta*, the last of which refers to the senate's decisions. The classic period added the jurisconsults' opinions, which organized the entire field.

Quintus Mucius Scaevola is the first jurisconsult who wrote extensively about law. He can be recognized as the initiator of the classic period. The young Marcus Tullius Cicero was his pupil, and Cicero praised Scaevola's great knowledge of the law. In spite of that, Cicero still favored his friend Servius Sulpicius Rufus as the initiator of legal science.[1]

> "Precisely like that, Brutus," I say, "I consider that Scaevola and many others have had considerable practice in regards to civil law but it was Sulpicius and only Sulpicius who turned it into science, the type of science that would have never gotten to the knowledge of the law itself, if he had not learned the science that teaches how to divide the parts of a whole, the science that explains what is hidden by defining it, that enlightens what is dark by interpreting it, to see all the ambiguities and then detail them and finally to possess a rule to be able to judge what is true and what is false, and to define which are the consequences that can be extracted and the ones that cannot, given certain premises. He applied this science, the most important of all, almost like a light thrown over those issues that were confusedly treated by others in the legal processes and in the opinions."
> "It seems to me you are alluding to the dialectic," he said.
> "I am, in fact," I responded, "but he added the knowledge of the letters and the elegance of the word, something that one can easily spot in his writings, which do not have comparison" (Cicero, 1923:, 152, 153)[2]

Historians of Roman law generally consider that the classic period goes from the first century BC to the beginning of the third century AD.[3] It coincided with the great Mediterranean expansion of Roman power and with the political period called the Principate (27 BC to AD 235), a time when the republican institutions were maintained, but the real political power was concentrated in the emperors. The intellectual elaboration of the jurisconsults transformed the law of a city attached to old customs and ancestral ways into a broader law that responded to business needs. Roman law was able to expand in this new universe, not only because of the power of Rome, which did not in fact impose its law formally, but also because of the intellectual qualities of the law's elaboration (Frier, 1985; Schiavone, 2009).

From Cicero's account of his experience as Scaevola's pupil, we have a good picture of how instruction in Roman law took place at the beginning of the classic period. Young men lived at a jurisconsult's house.[4] In the morning they accompanied him to receive clients and other citizens who wished to pay their respects and hear his opinions.[5] Later, the young men would follow the jurisconsult to the forum (the market square), where they heard his opinions. In the afternoon they would discuss the different cases and events of the day. This education was not meant as training for future jurisconsults; rather, it was expected that the elite citizen of Rome possessed a basic understanding of the law. Cicero himself did not become a jurisconsult. Instead, he became a very distinguished speaker, writer, thinker, and politician. In other words, this education was very general and informal. It was also socially selective, restricted to a jurisconsult's relatives or close friends whom he was willing to receive into his own home. Aside from Cicero, Scaevola was a teacher to a number of jurisconsults (Domingo, 2004:6).

A more formal education became possible only once the law was consolidated as an intellectual discipline, primarily due to the organization of legal knowledge by the first jurisconsults during the early classic period. The jurisconsult Labeon (43 BC to AD 20), who lived during the time of Augustus, dedicated several hours during the day to conversing with young men, but nothing has survived of his teachings. Masurio Sabino (first century AD) was probably the first to merit the title of law professor. In contrast with Scaevola, Sulpicius, and other jurisconsults who were patricians of the senatorial class, Sabino had modest social origins. He was intellectually brilliant, which caught the attention of the emperor Tiberius, and thanks to the emperor's support, he managed to ascend to the equestrian order. Most likely, his modest social origins allowed him to dedicate part of his time to the formal education of young men, a task considered improper for a person with high social status (Schulz, 1946:55–59).

In the history of Roman law, Sabino is known as the founder of a school designated as "Sabinian," in his honor. It is likely that Sabino wrote a book for teaching law, but nothing of it has survived. In addition to the Sabinians, there was the Proculian school, whose origin dates back to Labeon (Schulz, 1946:119). Although we know little about these schools (Riggsby, 2010:57–66), they clearly were not academic institutions as we know them today. There are even discussions of what the word "school" meant in this context. Most likely, they involved gatherings in which a person who knew the law to some extent gave explanations to people who were less informed. Education in these schools was informal in the sense that it was not recognized institutionally, and the professors received no reward or payment for their teaching. In fact, the great jurisconsult Ulpian warned that the law was a type of knowledge so prestigious that one could not charge for teaching it because in doing so, one would commodify it and consequently reduce its prestige (Chroust, 1954:518).

The apprentices or students were young people who already had a prior education in grammar, rhetoric, and arithmetic. Instruction in rhetoric often included problems and analysis related to the law. As a result, students had basic knowledge about the law. They were also well informed about history and myths (Marrou, 1981). Most likely, the educational activities took place at the professor's house or in a temple. It was only during the second century AD that the city of Rome designated a special classroom (*auditoria publica*) at professors' disposal (Chroust, 1954).

It is not completely clear how the jurisconsults influenced the transformation of the legal field. Aulus Gellius, an intellectual who served as *iudex* in many cases, wrote a commendation of the jurisconsults' writings. In it he praised the jurisconsults' learnedness in the fields of grammar and rhetoric (Howley, 2013) and argued that the cultured citizen could benefit from reading their work. However, he gave no indication that judges cited the jurisconsults' work.[6] The jurisconsults' writing was apparently nontechnical, very different from the literature produced by law professors today. In the postclassic period these writings became the center of legal education. It is likely that this use started during the final centuries of the Principate.

The first didactic work that we know of related to the law is called the *Institutes*. Its author, Gaius (active AD 130–180), also wrote other types of work about the law. During his time, he was not mentioned as a jurisconsult, and we know very little about his life. He did not have the prestige of high social status (he most likely came from a province). Only later did his opinions gain a great reputation. The *Institutes* is a textbook containing a summary of the main rules of the law. It seems to have served as a vademecum, or guidebook, for learning but apparently was put to little use for the practice of law during the classic era (Coing, 1959:30).

There was growth of legal education in the postclassic period, but little has come down to us regarding the educational activities or content of the curriculum. It is likely that students engaged in discussions of cases and the work of jurisconsults, which was focused on specific situations and well-founded problems. In any case, it appears safe to say that the relative formalization of legal education coincided with a more substantial intellectual elaboration of the law (Evêque, 2019). Some call it the birth of the law as a science (Villey,1964:37). Notably, the first law school in a more modern sense was established not in Rome but in Beirut at the beginning of the third century (Atkinson, 1970).[7] At the beginning of the fifth century, a law school was founded in Constantinople. By this time, there were a number of very small law schools in several cities, each with perhaps two or three salaried professors and a modest number of students. According to Chroust (1954:521), after a few years of instruction, the students took an examination, but Chroust does not cite a document or testimony to support this.

Thanks to Justinian, we know the curriculum of law schools during the fifth century. Students completed the program in four to five years. In the first year, they studied Gaius's *Institutes* and a big part of Ulpian's *Libri ad Sabinum*. They studied dowries, custodies, testaments, and legacies. Instruction in the second year focused on procedural subjects, among others, mostly derived from Ulpian's work. In the third year, students covered Papinian's answers (opinions), and in the fourth year, the answers of Paul. Finally, in the fifth year, they studied the imperial constitutions.

In the sixth century, Justinian reformed legal education. He established a new curriculum based on the *Corpus Iuris Civilis*, which also took as its starting point the *Institutes* (Jolowicz & Nicholas, 1972:498–499). We do not know which teaching methods were used, but given the reading materials, the consideration of specific situations was likely a key approach. Only the *Institutes* focused more on the rules themselves, but even it made frequent reference to specific situations.

Under Justinian, the occupation of professors began to gain more prestige. They were well paid and given public honors. Law professors in Constantinople were placed in charge of the great compilation ordered by Justinian (Chroust, 1954:528). Justinian recognized only three institutions for legal education: Rome, Beirut, and Constantinople, surely because he was concerned about the quality of legal education elsewhere. At that time, there were four professors in Constantinople and four in Beirut. In Rome, law education probably had declined.

It is clear that Justinian wanted to reestablish the splendor of the Roman Empire as well as of the law. He launched military conquests and major construction projects. He had successfully achieved partial reunification of the Roman Empire when an epidemic interrupted his plans. The Italian region was the most successful reconquest insofar as it maintained a Byzantine presence until the ninth century. However, Justinian's most enduring work was the great compilation that is known as the *Corpus Iuris Civilis*. He used tradition as a foundation of this work. The *Digest*, which is a very important part of the *Corpus*, consists of excerpts from the classical jurisconsults' writings (not without some changes, called interpolations). The *Institutes* was also a very important part of the *Corpus*. It was an enlarged edition of Gaius's work and bore the same name. The *Corpus* also contained the *Code* and the *Novels*, which were compilations of the emperors' work.

Justinian wanted his work to be comprehensive and definitive. He therefore ordered the burning of all previous works on law and mandated that the *Corpus* not be modified. This type of restorative conservation in fact changed the concept of law. The writings of the jurisconsults were the opinions of private people; they had *auctoritas* but lacked power. The jurisconsults' opinions were based on their knowledge and experience. That type of knowledge had been developing over time, and the jurisconsults found ways to organize it and adapt it to new circumstances. With the *Corpus Iuris Civilis*, the law became a written document, sanctioned by the existing political power, that settled the rules. According to Justinian's conception, any type of change was inconceivable. In other words, when the work and writings of the jurisconsults were hypostatized, the nature of the law changed. The work and writings were treated as settled foundational principles. The law was dissociated from experience and was not susceptible to change with the evolving needs of society. Curiously, the *Corpus* was promulgated by a political power and sought to establish the law once and for all. In the future, however, it would be disconnected from political power and from social change as well. This work clearly blocked adaptation and innovation.

This new conception of the law also changed legal education. From a rather informal process of discussing opinions related to experience and specific situations, legal education shifted to focus on a static written text.

The very concept of a fixed written law was an illusion, however. Lived experience entered indirectly because the jurisconsults' texts referenced specific situations and generally explained the origin and convenience (or justice) of a rule. Despite the effort to establish an unchanging body of law for students to master, the process of explaining and discussing the texts required building an understanding, and because a text is always reconstructed by the varied interpretations of its readers, it is likely that individual and social experiences and changing circumstances were re-introduced into consideration. Justinian's ambition succumbed to reality. Centuries later the *Corpus* was broadly commented on and had an un-expected fate and astonishing importance, which is treated in the next section.

THE LAW IN THE UNIVERSITIES

The great humanitarian catastrophe that was the ancient world's decay affected the life of law and the continuity of its study in what is now Europe. In the post-Justinian period and the early Middle Ages, efforts were made to continue with legal education in Ravena and Pavia (Ca-lasso, 1954:267ss; Gualazzini, 1974) as well as in Constantinople. These efforts encountered many obstacles because of the difficult times in which people lived (Bréhier, 1926). The extant literature mentions a small number of professors with minimal intellectual production. We know almost nothing about the numbers and quality of their students, but we assume they were few. Given the difficult conditions of life during this period, it is perhaps more surprising and admirable that the field of law and its understanding survived at all.

The *Corpus Iuris Civilis* did not have a major impact in the Western Roman Empire because the Byzantine conquests had only transient in-fluence there, except in the area of Ravenna (the Exarchate of Ravenna), which maintained Byzantine rule until the eighth century. In the sev-enth century, the expansion of Islam and Arabic civilization into North Africa and a good part of the Iberian Peninsula considerably reduced the Byzantine Empire. In the Mediterranean, navigation was no longer safe, and, in general, communication became more difficult. Within the Byzantine Empire, the Justinian compilation had limited impact in part

because it was written in Latin in a region where Greek was the predominant language. Some partial Greek versions were written in attempts
to increase its relevance (Jolowicz & Nicholas, 1972:500–515). During
the early Middle Ages, the *Corpus Iuris Civilis* definitely did not play the
central role in the law and the society that Justinian had envisioned. The
work, which was intended to restore the law and establish it forever, separate from changes in political power, had neither the diffusion nor the
impact that Justinian hoped for.

Nevertheless, law studies did not disappear entirely. For instance,
Rome maintained a law school, although we know little beyond that.
In Pavia there were studies of Lombard and Roman law, but they were
probably at a relatively basic level. The study of rhetoric and a certain
level of legal knowledge were maintained, but eventually that knowledge
lost importance (Koschaker, 1955). Knowledge became theocentric and
a new concept of the law emerged (García Pelayo, 1962) that had little
impact on legal education, whose decline is generally acknowledged
(Koschaker, 1955).

At the end of the eleventh century this situation changed. In Europe,
a period of prosperity and cultural blossoming began, generally referred
to as the Renaissance of the twelfth century (Verger, 1996). In addition,
the Crusades resulted in political and military expansion. Centers for
study were created and enjoyed certain privileges; the universities began
to take shape. These institutions assumed responsibility for all the instruction passed down from ancient times, which was regarded as fundamental. These included the trivium (grammar, dialectic, and rhetoric)
and the quadrivium (arithmetic, geometry, astronomy, and music). Two
intellectual disciplines, theology and law, were considered especially important and were the main medieval additions to knowledge and education. In terms of theological studies, knowledge took the form of the
revealed word of God, mainly in the Gospels but also in the Old Testa-
ment and the writings of the church fathers. In terms of the law, the main
text was the *Corpus Iuris Civilis*, which was viewed as encompassing all
knowledge of the law since ancient times (Le Goff, 1985).

When the *Corpus Iuris Civilis* was taken as an object of study, medieval
scholars applied methods of understanding and interpretation that we
now understand as Scholastic. Law became a discipline linked directly

to universities. The University of Bologna is a prime example and is considered very important for the birth and development of law studies (Calasso, 1954; Stelling-Michaud, 1955; Wieacker, 1980:I,62–69). There, a group of professors (glossators) made the *Corpus Iuris Civilis,* especially the *Digest,* the center of attention. The glossators were university professors whose knowledge was widely admired, for good reason. Justinian's *Corpus* is a complex work that includes fragments of very important authors from the classic Roman period. Often these authors took opposing positions on key issues. The Constantinople professors who originally compiled the jurisconsults' opinions had attempted to eliminate such contradictions, but their efforts were far from perfect because of the time pressure Justinian had imposed on completion of their work. Their changes and additions (called interpolations) sometimes made comprehending the text still more complex (Koschaker, 1955:101ss; Brundage, 2008).

The study of canon law, or the law of the Catholic Church, was soon added to the university curriculum. The bishop and jurist Ivo de Chartres (later St. Ivo), who lived in the second half of the eleventh century (c. 1040–1116), was very important in the conception of the field and organization of these rules (Grossi, 2010:17–19). The study at the universities was done using a document compilation made by the jurist Benedictine monk Gratian (Gratianus, c. 1100–1159) This work was called the *Decree* or *Decretum Gratiani* (its formal name was *Concordia discordatium canonum*); it was a compilation that included decisions of popes and holy councils, together with selected texts of the church fathers and, above all, the Gospels themselves (Villey, 1962:189–201).

In the universities, the text from Justinian or Gratian required formal presentation and explanation. Given that a copy from the original manuscript would have been prohibitively expensive, teaching started with dictation from the text. The wealthiest students had a type of secretary who was tasked with writing the copy, but the other students made their own. The teachers were in charge of reading and explaining the text, a process known as the *lectio. Lecture* in English, *lección* in Spanish, and *leçon* in French all derive from the word *lectio,* but the *lectio* was not an independent explanation given by the professor; it was more of a reading with commentary. The text had authority in itself, and the professor's job was only to clarify it. The explanation was summarized and written beside the main text and is known as the *glosa*. For this reason, the professors were referred to as glossators (Stelling-Michaud, 1955).

Many divergent texts could be found regarding the same subject, and it was not easy to find the most relevant one. To address these issues, the professor organized discussion with the students so they could understand the basis of the divergency (the *sic et non*). The professor intervened to make the *determinatio*, explaining the meaning of the divergences and finding ways to reconcile them. This phase of instruction was the dispute, or *questio*. The professors wrote summaries of these disputes and published them in *summas*, or aggregations of questions. These educational activities involving the *lectio* took place in the early morning. During the afternoon, students engaged in less formalized and directed activities, including disputes and organized debates for the discussion of cases and problems of interpretation that had been identified. The latter activities offered a less systematic experience of the law (Coing, 1959:31).

The law school in Bologna soon transformed into a university in which the law itself was central. Students from throughout Europe traveled there to study. Despite the general struggles of life in a new city that was ill prepared to receive the growing number of students and the enormous difficulties and costs of transportation, books, and professor's fees, which came directly from students, a significant number of students enrolled. During the thirteenth century, annual enrollment ranged between five hundred and one thousand law students, grouped together in "nations" by their region of origin (Stelling-Michaud, 1955). The medieval facilities built to house some of these nations still stand in Bologna.

The educational method developed in Bologna spread via universities throughout Europe and eventually to Spanish America. At the beginning of the thirteenth century, a considerable number of lawyers, judges, and notaries received university law education under this model of instruction. Formal admission to the profession and an oath to observe ethical behavior were introduced. The number of professionals grew rapidly (Brundage, 2008:4). The success of the universities was notable and rapid.

An important question is why Roman law achieved such great prestige and success in the medieval world and why a text as complex as the *Corpus Iuris Civilis* became the center of its study. Many possible explanations have been offered. A common one is that Roman law is intrinsically superior, but this argument is hard to accept for those who view the law within a social context. In the latter view, there is no perfect or superior law but only a law that is more or less appropriate to social needs. Another explanation is related to the new needs resulting from the commerce and active exchange of European life during the eleventh century. This argument is also unsatisfying because there is no certainty that the complex text, which by the twelfth century had become rather old and difficult to understand, served the needs of economic activity. Padoa-Schioppa (2017:73–81) offers another and more convincing argument that the needs of economic life forced people to overcome customary law, which was local, and to seek a common law that served a broader space. Roman law was the option available.

Koschaker (1955) offers explanations based on political and cultural forces. He argues that the emperor of the Holy Roman Empire had an interest in using Roman traditional knowledge to establish his superior power, given that he presented himself as the successor of the Roman emperors. For this reason, he gave all the support he could to universities and professors of Roman law. The emperor had rivals, however, including the popes, who also aspired to attain supreme power, and the kings, who were willing to accept neither the pope's nor the emperor's tutelage but who could ally themselves with one or the other. For this reason, the very teaching of Roman law was controversial. At the University of Paris it was forbidden, largely because of the coalition between the king of France and the pope against the emperor.[8] As a consequence, the University of Paris distinguished itself for its theology and canon law studies but not for Roman law. Focusing on these actors is a political explanation. Ultimately, the cultural prestige of ancient Rome overcame such resistance. A compilation of the Roman knowledge regarding law was difficult to ignore; this is a cultural explanation. The association between Roman law and the empire soon blurred as jurists elaborated the concept of sovereignty and emphasized that the king was an emperor in his kingdom. In this way, they managed to draw the king to their side.

A different explanation focuses on the benefits of the disciplined study required of the students of Roman law. Those who successfully completed their studies learned to read carefully and to interpret and handle written texts; they learned to make distinctions and reason coherently. The effects of the study of Roman law gradually shaped and strengthened the very justifications for requiring it. Whatever the reasons for the attraction of Roman law, jurists became very useful in the exercise of power.

In the late Middle Ages people began to perceive a change in those who wielded power. Instead of armed men on horseback, strong and sun-burned, with scars and ragged clothes, they were desk people, haggard and pale, with clothes that were threadbare at the elbows because of their constant writing and the many hours they worked at their desk. They were men of the law, the bureaucracy, a word derived from *bureau*, or "desk," in French (Maravall, 1972:II,443–472).

The successors of the glossators were the commentators (others called them post-glossators). These professors followed the same method of contrasting the various sources and then arriving at a conclusion that integrated different authorities, but the commentators also relied on broader sources than Roman law, especially the statutes of the cities. Consequently, they made great effort to adapt Roman law to the needs of their time (Stelling-Michaud, 1955:52–61). Glossators and commentators constituted the so-called *mos italicus*, because most of the professors were Italian or had been educated in Italy, especially in Bologna and later in Perugia, where Bartolo de Sassoferrato (1313–1357), the most famous of the commentators, taught. In this manner, the teaching method of Roman law, developed first in Italy, spread throughout Europe. Universities were founded in various cities of Italy, France, Germany, Spain, England, and Portugal. The number of law students grew rapidly.

Professors taught in Latin, and they did so in different European regions, regardless of their place of birth or training. Among Italian legal scholars, Placentinus established Roman law studies at Montpelier, and Vacarius taught at Oxford, both in the twelfth century. Azo taught in Provence in the thirteenth century. The French professors Hotman and Doneau also taught Roman law, the former in Switzerland and England, and the latter in Germany. However, these French professors were part not of the *mos italicus* but of the *mos gallicus*, or the French way of teaching and dealing with Roman law, which will be discussed later.

The role that professors had was very important from the twelfth to the sixteenth century. They were not purely bookish men; they were also able to answer queries from emperors, kings, and lords, and they could serve government functions as judges or ambassadors. In general, they participated actively in practical life. The law had been transformed into written text, but professors were responsible for interpreting it and were aware of and attentive to the needs of everyday life (Brundage, 2008; Stelling-Michaud, 1955). The Roman law that predominated in Europe during the late Middle Ages and for much of the modern era came from the interpreted texts (or transformed texts) developed by professors (Piano Mortari, 1976). This was the European *ius commune* (Grossi, 2010; Koschaker, 1955).

Legal education also included canon law. Gratian's *Decretum* (twelfth century), which was a compilation of canons, constituted the basis for the teaching of canon law. The *Decretum* was later accompanied by other documents to form a new compilation called the *Corpus Iuris Canonici.* Studying Roman law was considered fundamental for the understanding of canon law, although the Gospels are the most frequent citations in the *Decretum* (Villey, 1962:189–201). Canon law was important for the development of family law and successions and in all matters regarding the organization of the Catholic Church. The canonists were not appreciated among the Romanists (Koschaker, 1955), but they had the support of the pope and the church. Legal studies included both types of law, although it was necessary to take an examination in only one of them. Students who took both examinations and graduated in both laws were doctors *utriusque juris.*

Thus, Roman law, supplemented by canon law and, above all, by the *summas* and glosses of the professors, became the common European law until the eighteenth century. This does not mean that the only applicable law was Roman law or canon law. Judges and functionaries had to apply local laws and customs. These were not formally taught, but thanks to the method of considering cases and authorities to find the just rule, jurists could incorporate local laws and merchants' customs, even though each of those legal systems had its own sources of legitimacy (Calasso, 1954:607–628.; Grossi, 2010).

From the twelfth century onward, university legal education spread throughout Europe. The list of universities that taught law grew long, and the number of students increased rapidly. The preparation of students and the duration of the courses varied in time and place. In Bologna, during the thirteenth century, students had to be prepared in Latin grammar, logic, and rhetoric to begin legal studies (Stelling-Michaud, 1955:66). Roman law was the center of all legal studies, although what was taught under that name naturally shifted according to the predominant ideas of the time (Koschaker, 1955). Canon law followed Roman law in importance. In general, little attention was paid to local law, but in Bologna the *Liber feudorom* was incorporated in instruction. In Castile and the Spanish colonies, special attention was paid to the *Siete Partidas*, a work elaborated during the reign of Alfonso X (1252–1284), although formally it was not a fundamental or required reading at the universities. The method of teaching also varied depending on the context.

These changes in legal education implied a change in the conception of law itself. In the classic period, when Roman law was developed, the law was intrinsically associated with lived experience. During the postclassic period, and especially under Justinian, law became a written text consecrated by political power. In the Middle Ages, law was a bookish knowledge because it was understood that all the law was contained in the writing of ancient authorities, especially in the *Corpus Iuris Civilis*. The study of law therefore focused on knowing how to read and interpret that great text, which no longer had political traction. The legitimacy of the text itself was centered on the fact that it was accepted as the main source of legal knowledge.

Justinian and the Roman emperors were historical figures with no political power in Bologna or anywhere else in twelfth- to fourteenth-century Europe. Likewise, the authority of the professors' comments, which helped to clarify the law and to make it applicable to concrete situations, did not derive from the approval of political powers. The emperors of the Holy Roman Empire assumed the body of legal knowledge as their own and encouraged its spread, but their power was limited. City governments, kings, and other lords could also promulgate rules, but those were not the core of the law and were not expected to change what was established as Roman law or natural law. Long-established custom also had to be respected. Legislators could only interpret and consolidate law or regulate something not previously established (Villey, 1988). Fundamentally, however, the law was the Roman law as established in the Justinian corpus and interpreted by professors and law graduates.

Until the eighteenth century, positive legislation did not have much importance but was taken into account as part of the law (Moccia, 1988).

It is important to highlight the knowledge, social position, and skills of the law graduates during this era. They belonged to the upper class of society. At a time when the majority of the population was illiterate, these men (they were all men) could read and express themselves orally and in writing, both in the vernacular language and in Latin. Their mastery of Latin, the language of God and justice, made them stand out. Jurists handled the ancient knowledge contained in books, to which very few people had access. They had the ability to articulate fine distinctions and to argue effectively. They also knew the *lex sacra*, the type of law that is most associated with religion and the church.

The professors, men familiar with the practice of law, adapted the ancient knowledge to the needs of their time (Stelling-Michaud, 1955:53). University studies were complemented by a period of internship that allowed the students to get to know every aspect of the profession and to become familiar with the local customs and regulations. Law, as a discipline, and thanks to a well-developed method, had succeeded in integrating theory and practice, the profane and the sacred, past and present. The jurists' knowledge was universal and did not depend on politics, but it was not abstract knowledge. It was wisdom well anchored in society and attentive to social needs. All this gave jurists a superior and privileged place in society.

BREEZES OF THE MODERN ERA

The intellectual environment of the Middle Ages was not tranquil. Commentaries had multiplied in number and variety. Rivalries between professors were open and pointed. At the end of the Middle Ages, a movement developed consisting predominantly of French Roman law scholars, or those who taught in France (the *mos gallicus*). These scholars were critical of the work of the glossators and commentators, and they included in their criticism Justinian's own *Digest*. Of course, they recognized the excellence of the great classic Roman jurists but argued that their contributions had grown cluttered and distorted in the compilation. The focus of the criticism was Tribonian, the intellectual jurist commissioned by

Justinian to make the compilation, but it also included the work of glossators and commentators. A sample of the severe criticism during late medieval times directed at these scholars can be seen in François Hotman's *Anti-Tribonianus* (or *Hotomanus*, in its Latin version, 1524–1590):

> The aforesaid four great doctors and counselors of the Emperor Frederick left in writing some glosses and small apostilles on the books of Justinian, and they were so imitated by their successors that in three hundred years they produced more treatises, disputations, commentaries, advices, decisions, observations, annotations, repetitions, exceptions, apostilles, and other writings, than during the prior fourteen hundred years. With this each of these doctors wanted to make himself known, to publish and to praise himself so as to be sought after by princes, called upon by the universities of law. . . .

> This provoked another unusual disgrace and, to tell the truth, abominable before God and before men . . . that there is no matter today in which there are no evident contradictions. . . .

> Thus there are some who claim to have warned that those who begin to study the books of Justinian too young and without having equipped and prepared their spirit with philosophy and good letters easily attempt against their intelligence . . . (Hotman, 1567/2013:171–172).

For the humanist jurists of the *mos gallicus*, the law remained embodied in the Roman texts, but they criticized the disorder of the Justinian compilation and the interpretive methods of the *mos italicus* jurists as having obscured the original meaning. They were, after all, humanists of the *via moderna*, and they viewed their immediate predecessors as part of the dark and barbaric medieval age. In the opinion of the humanists, the glossators and commentators lacked a good knowledge of classical Latin. The humanist criticism involved revealing the interpretive errors and spurious texts that had accrued over the years and searching for the lost rationality of the Roman law of the classic period, an idea that today's Roman law historians completely discount (Piano Mortari, 1978).

Humanist jurists showed a preference for the *Institutes* (in Justinian's version), which they found to be a much better ordered and simpler text than the *Digest*. As previously noted, the *Institutes* was an introductory text, and for that reason, it was clearer and easier to consult than other parts of the compilation. One of the great jurist-humanists, Cujas (Cujacius,

1522–1590) believed that the *Institutes* did not require any commentary (Beck Varela, 2013:56). The quality of this work made it the greatest didactic law text of the seventeenth to nineteenth centuries, but accompanied by the commentaries and annotations of humanist jurists, as we will see.

The culmination of the work of the humanists, later blended with the so-called natural law school (*iure naturae et gentium*), can be seen in the transformation of law itself and of the didactic literature. For example, Jean Domat (1625–1696) studied law at the University of Bourges with Edmond Mérille, one of Cujas's disciples. He was a jurist of the *mos gallicus* and a friend of Pascal, and he was involved in the birth of rationalist thought (Renoux-Zagamé, 2007). His great work, *Les lois civiles dans leur ordre naturel* (Domat, 1689), succeeded in organizing Roman law in its natural (or rational) order. It produced a transformation in the law. Note that this work is in French rather than Latin, a major departure from what was considered the language of the law during that time.

A reading of this brief work shows it to be very distant from the *Digest* or even from the summary of the rules of Roman law that are contained in the *Institutes* of Justinian. In its structure, style, and language, it is much closer to our civil codes. This is not a chance resemblance. Domat's work had a notable influence on the drafters of the *Code Civil des Français* (1804), which in turn influenced most modern civil codes, especially in Latin America. The idea of simplifying and drafting the rules of law in the national language and having them approved by the king was a common idea among humanist jurists. Domat's work and, ultimately, the Civil Code, constitute the culmination of that initial aspiration. However, Domat's purpose was not legislative; rather, he aspired to write a didactic work that would make Roman law more accessible.

Another influential instructional work was the edition of Justinian's *Institutes* with commentary by Arnold Vinnius (or Vinnio, 1588–1657), formally called *In quator libros Institutionum imperialium commentarius academicus et forensis* (1642). Vinnius was a student of Tunning and indirectly of Doneau (Donellus, 1527–1591), both representatives of the *mos gallicus*. He was a professor at Leiden and author of a number of well-known books on Roman law. His commented edition of the *Institutes* became the equivalent of a bestseller and was adopted as a textbook for the teaching of civil law in Europe and Spanish America. In 1726 the jurist-philosopher Johan Gottlieb Heineccius added some annotations that have accompanied it ever since. Between 1642 and 1867 hundreds of editions of the Vinnius *Institutes* were printed. This book was known in Spain and Spanish America as "el Vinnio." Beck Varela (2013) devoted a work of more than six hundred pages to it in which she recounts and analyzes the vicissitudes of this book in Spain, where it was published during the eighteenth and nineteenth centuries. Vinnius was a Calvinist, and the circulation of his book in Catholic Spain required that it be censored ("punished") in those passages that could be considered heterodox. In the nineteenth century it was translated into modern languages, among them Spanish (Beck Varela, 2013).

In short, thanks to the work of people like Domat and Vinnius, Roman law was converted into a rational system. Leibniz considered Roman law to be the *ratio scripta*, or written reason, and legal scholars were intent on discovering its rational order, just as scientists were finding the laws of nature (Martínez Tapia, 1996). Savigny used the same expression, and he thought that Roman jurists made calculations comparable to those of Euclid (Coing, 1959). Each author made efforts to improve the systematization of Roman law. This is what Heineccius set out to do in his work on ancient Roman law (*Antiquitatum romanorum jurisprudentiam ilustrantium sintagma*, 1718), which became a university text for the study of rational Roman law.

Parallel to the conversion of Roman law into a rational system, an independent systematization was being developed, the so-called school of natural law and law of nations. This systematization originated outside the universities but was later incorporated as an additional professorship. Grotius (1583–1645) is reputed to be the initiator of this trend of thought, and numerous authors can be linked to this school. These two ways of approaching rationalization of the law have different origins but do not conflict. Vinnius incorporated fragments of Grotius in his comments to the *Institutes*. Heineccius, in addition to adding notes to Vinnius's book, published his work on the systematization of Roman law, already mentioned, and a work on natural law and the law of nations (*Elementa iuris natura et gentium*, 1737).

One of the main functions of the numerous editions of Vinnius's work was the incorporation of national law, which was one of the main themes legal authors had wrestled with since the sixteenth century. In general, the aim was to show that national law coincided with Roman law, except in certain matters of details. Of course, there were some difficulties regarding the determination of national law to include in Vinnius's work. For example, Juan de Sala edited the *Vinnius castigatus* in 1779, one of his purposes being the incorporation of Hispanic law. Basically, he drew on the *Siete Partidas*, which by the eighteenth and nineteenth centuries was regarded as ancient Castilian law. This use of Castilian law as national law annoyed the Catalans, so an edition of Vinnius was published in Barcelona in 1846, in which references to the law of Catalonia were added. However, the book was published in Spanish (Beck Varela, 2013:636). Publication in languages more accessible than Latin was an aspiration of the time.

The insistence on focusing on national law raised a new issue. National law is that approved by the will of the sovereign. What happens if the national law and the natural law differ. What is the true law? Those who put the accent on natural law were called jusnaturalists, and those who put the accent on the national (positive) law were called juspositivists. The juspositivists began dismissing natural law as "metaphysics," but the factions shared the idea that the purpose was to build a rational system of law.

The systematization of the law transformed legal knowledge. The main method of gaining knowledge was to locate the axiomatic principles and from there to deduce the whole content of the law. In addition, the rules of national law have to be integrated in this system. Deductive reasoning thus replaced the medieval or Scholastic dialectic, which was the opposition of authorities in order to draw the most satisfactory conclusion. The legal discipline became a "geometric" science based on principles dictated by reason and enshrined by the legislator.

This new conception of law and legal knowledge, and the new type of literature, had an impact on the way the law was taught, although the changes in teaching methods were slow to develop and varied by country. The first change was the relative liberation from the text. Professors did not consider it necessary for courses to cover the entire *Digest*, but they began to concentrate on those parts that were of practical interest; they focused on what was relevant to the current society. After some time,

Justinian's *Institutes* became the fundamental text and was most likely accompanied by the additional explanations by the professor. Much later, in the nineteenth century, the lecture entirely replaced readings and debates, which made the transmission of systematized information easier. Another important change was the emphasis on national law, expressed in the national language. In France there was a major reform in 1679 under the aegis of Louis XIV. As part of this reform, the royal chair of French law was instituted. The professors in charge of this teaching had a complicated task because French national law did not exist. There were local or regional customs with important differences between regions of France, and existing systematization was minimal (Kuskowski, 2022). Unlike the other professors, who taught in Latin, professors of French law had to teach in French. This reform did not have a major impact on the universities (Curzon, 1919), perhaps because the professors were not particularly distinguished, with the exception of Robert Joseph Pothier (1699–1772). He truly stood out as a law professor and became a reference point in French legal thought during the eighteenth and nineteenth centuries. He was a perceptive and thorough reader of natural law, and as professor of French law, he was very familiar with regional customs. He looked for the common elements in those customs and expressed them in precise language (Halpérin, 2009; Thireau, 2007). His most important works (*Traité des obligations*, 1761, and later monographs on various contracts) were written in French.

The pace of change in the conception and teaching of law increased following the French Revolution, which produced a massive reorganization of French society and of Europe in general. In France, the revolution flattened the social hierarchy, society became more homogeneous, and local privileges disappeared. France became politically unified, and the people became equal citizens; these changes facilitated the simplification and systematic reorganization of the law. The result was the legal code in its modern sense. The code constitutes a brief book of systematically organized legal rules, promulgated by the political authority, and relevant to the whole state. Napoleon himself took a personal interest in the elaboration of the French Civil Code. The code repeals all previous legal rules in the area it regulates, thus further simplifying the law (Tarello, 1988:41–60 ; 1976).

The code made the Enlightenment project possible. The code was the product of reason, expressed in national language, and it was supported by the political power or the state (Halpérin, 1992). The origins of the code are found in the literature produced by humanist jurisprudence and the school of natural law (Arnaud, 1969; Caroni 2013). Pothier's work had a profound influence, as evidenced by the fact that about a quarter of the articles of the French code can be traced directly to his work (Pothier, 1845). In other words, the origin is doctrinal, understood as part of the intellectual elaboration of the law that took place in the seventeenth and eighteenth centuries (Halpérin, 2009). The process of elaboration during the revolutionary period was turbulent (Halpérin, 1992), and only when the revolution was over (according to its drafters) was its completion possible (Portalis, 1801). Defining the codes as the centerpieces of the law transformed the discipline of law and required rethinking legal education.

When the whole branch of the law is assumed to be contained in a code, we return to the conception of all the law as contained in an authoritative written record, the same idea that was the foundation of Justinian's project. All the prior literature became irrelevant or acquired a purely historical interest. Unlike the Justinian *Corpus*, a code is not a compilation but a systematic arrangement, supposedly a product of reason. At the same time, a code is promulgated by the political power and carries with it the threat of coercion by the state. Since a code is supposed to govern society, the codifiers take into account the previous law and customs, but once promulgated, the law is only what a code establishes. This was considered the pinnacle of the evolution of the law, the systematization and rationalization of all law (Grossi, 2010:93–117). As a consequence, the intellectual work related to the code consists largely of commentary on its articles.

Such commentary is very important because it resolves doubts about the scope or meaning of a specific article of the code. It is both scientific and practical in terms of guiding the practice of the law. The scientific task is to interpret the articles, for which purpose textual analysis must be applied to determine the proper meaning of the words. This is the grammatical or literal interpretation. In case of persistent doubt, the interpreter can resort to systematic interpretation, that is, placing the article in the conceptual system of the code. An interpreter who wants to display erudition can resort to historical analysis, but this is considered outside the realm of rigorous science. The center of attention must be the text itself (Tarello, 1988:69–101). In France, the jurists who interpreted the codes were called *l'école de l'exégèse*; they were jurists who functioned independently of one another, despite their designation as an *école*, or school. The task of law professors also changed with the move to define law in terms of the civil code. Their mission was to teach students the codes, not the law in a broader sense. Reflecting this new focus of instruction, Bugnet, a professor in Paris, is credited with the phrase "je ne connais pas le droit civil, j'enseigne le Code Napoléon" (Halpérin, 2007).[9] Teaching thus became quite tedious. Because the scientific character of the law required that the meaning and subject of each article had to be explained, teachers did not have to be—perhaps could not be—too imaginative. There was no place for discussion. A law student in Paris during 1840 provides vivid pictures in his correspondence of the immense annoyance of the classes and their stultifying character. We know these letters because their author later became a famous writer: Gustave Flaubert (Le Bos, 2019).[10]

By examining the massive treatises explaining the codes, historians of law have worked to rescue the contribution of these professor-authors from their image as tedious and unimaginative. In their written explanations, they freely referenced various sources and sought to further systematize the law. They also published commentaries on judicial decisions that subsequently became influential (Hakim, 2005), but it seems that students did not appreciate their classes. As we will see, the dictatorship of the code did not last. Professors, judges, and lawyers gained independence and acquired an important place in French society (Arnaud, 1975).

The codes and exegetes, or commentators on the codes, not only changed French law but also had an important influence in other countries of Europe and Latin America, where codes and exegetes also developed (Caroni, 2013; Guzmán Brito, 2000; Tarello, 1988). Arnaud (1973) has criticized the idea of the rationality of the code and the scientific claims of its commentators, insisting on the ideological character of the enterprise. Even so, the codes nevertheless dominated the legal scene for more than a hundred years in the civil law tradition. What is of particular interest here is the idea that by making the professor's task the explanation of the codes, legal education was greatly impoverished. The educational philosopher and legal scholar Giner de los Ríos (1889) was a critic of Spanish legal education—he considered it superficial—at the end of the nineteenth century. The professor was limited to lecturing before an ever-growing number of students, generally repeating information contained in the textbook and in the code. The central issue in education was memorization sufficient to pass the examination, which took the law entirely out of its social context. This focus failed to allow students to cultivate other skills or to present intellectual challenge.

German legal education, as analyzed by Wieacker (1980:311–320), has a quite different history. In fact, in the seventeenth and eighteenth centuries, Germany did not exist as a unified nation. There were universities in different kingdoms or regions that competed among themselves to attract professors and students. This produced a variety of methods and styles and a lively intellectual discourse. At the beginning of the nineteenth century, codification was rejected, most likely as a reflection of the influence of Gustav Hugo (1764–1844) and Friedrich Karl von Savigny (1779–1861), who offered a different understanding of the science of law. Hugo was an accredited Romanist who rejected the philosophy of law as an analysis of legal principles (as developed in Germany by Kant, Fichte, and Hegel) and argued for a philosophy of positive law, which for him meant Roman law as practiced in Germany. Savigny developed that line of thought and was enormously influential both through his work and through his position as rector of the University of Berlin. The assumption was that Roman law was the *ratio scripta* and, consequently, a system of concepts could be built upon it (Becchi, 2009; Halpérin, 2015). This process started not with axioms but with principles observed in the living law.

German universities became active centers of legal research, research that also extended to ancient customary law. Professors were scholars and relied on a large academic staff to assist them in both research and teaching. The latter was enriched by the discussion of research and legal problems and situations. German professors created a new science of law by building a system of concepts and, at the same time, attending to historical scholarship. This trend became hugely influential throughout

Europe (Halpérin, 2015:176–177). Graduates provided the state with educated and well-prepared civil servants, as legal education was viewed as operating more in the interest of the state than of individuals and business (Wieacker, 1980:II,133–135). In this period, Germany became a state of jurists (Halpérin, 2015).

At the end of the nineteenth century, the German style came to predominate in Europe and Latin America. German authors were translated into Italian and Spanish, which facilitated their diffusion in the Latin world, and German authors were also widely read in central and eastern Europe. German universities and professors attracted students from many countries. Italy was influenced by German legal science at an early stage. A number of Italian jurists made conceptual doctrinal elaborations in the nineteenth or early twentieth century, as was the case for Scialoja (1856–1933), Giuseppe Chiovenda (1872–1934), and Francesco Carnelutti (1879–1965) (Brutti, 2011; Grossi, 2000; Rotondi, 1976). What characterized the Italian professors was the combination of academic activity with outstanding political involvement and advocacy (Malatesta, 2011). In the final decades of the nineteenth century, French professors were finally freed from following the order of the code in their teaching. Marcel Planiol (1853–1931) was the first to write a systematic treatise on civil law, followed within a few years by Ambroise Colin and Henri Capitant (Savatier, 1976). In general, universities, but especially the University of Paris, were placed at the center of the renewal of legal culture (Audren & Halpérin, 2013:111; Halpérin, 2011).

What may be termed the "conceptual treatment of the law" does not hesitate to draw on historical sources and allows for a personal, often controversial elaboration of the law. It is likely that the lectures of professors offering such systematic elaborations were more appealing than those of professors limiting themselves to exegeses, although the communication abilities of the professor were probably more significant for their popularity than the disciplinary conception of the law. The prestige of a professor rested on the quality and erudition of his writings and on the eloquence of his lectures.

At the end of the nineteenth century, both the exegetical and the conceptual treatment of the law were subject to intense criticism in Germany and France. Instead, the emphasis shifted to the purpose of the law (what we today would call the public policy aims) and the element of struggle to achieve goals and ensure rights. In the Germanic region, Rudolf von Jhering (1818–1892) was a Romanist and law philosopher who shook the intellectual environment at the end of the century with these ideas. Eugen Ehrlich (1862–1922) paid special attention to the social element involved in the creation of the law. He is considered one of the founders of the sociology of law (or law and society studies). In France, François Gény (1861–1959) developed a rigorous and severe critique of the exegesis and the conceptual constructions. His work regarding methods of interpretation and sources of law (Gény, 1899) was highly regarded in his time.

Ehrlich (1936:7–10) criticized German legal education to prepare judges, lawyers, and civil servants because it assumed that it was sufficient for them to know the rules of law. He praised the English approach, which included attention to litigation and to what is known today as transactional law. By pointing out that the law should not only be sought in the rules of the state or in judges' decisions, he paved the way for applying social science research to the life of the law. His ideas on research and legal education had little impact in Germany and elsewhere in Europe, or in Latin America, but he found an audience in the United States.[11]

In the long run, these critiques had an important impact on legal scholarship, highlighting the relation of the law with its social and historical context and, in that sense, modifying the conception of law. In contrast, the impact of these shifts in thinking on legal education in the form of new approaches has been much slower to develop. To a large extent, didactic literature still consists of manuals, which basically convey an organized view of the rules of the law (Jamin, 2011). Until the mid-twentieth century, most countries in the civil law tradition looked to the Paris Law School, with its thousands of students and highly accredited professors, as the model to follow. The instruction necessarily consisted of a large lecture hall, a prepared lecture delivered by the professor, and the publication of the lecture for the students to read as instructional material. These methods were later perceived as insufficient, so they were complemented in the second half of the twentieth century with *travaux pratiques* (practical works), relatively small groups led by assistants (Audren & Halpérin, 2013; Halpérin, 2011, 2021).

Pérez Lledó (2003:199) has observed that most Spanish professors pay little attention to their teaching obligations because they consider research and publication more important. This assertion is probably valid for Europe as a whole. In Latin America, most professors are also lawyers, judges, or public servants, and their professional obligations demand their attention. This lack of interest in legal education is also noted in works on European legal history (e.g., Herzog, 2018; Lesaffer, 2009). To this day, works related to legal scholarship or legal studies focus their attention on the ideas and on the professors' published work, but they ignore legal education and the institutional structures in which the works are produced (e.g., Grossi, 1986, 2000).

We will see later that in Latin America, the interest in legal education and its reform began relatively early in the twentieth century and intensified toward the last half of that century. Europe, with more consolidated structures, began later. These topics are discussed in the following chapters.

LATIN AMERICA IN THE HISPANIC PERIOD

Very early in the period of conquest and colonization of the Americas, the Spanish authorities established universities there. The curriculum included the general studies that came down from the Middle Ages, as well as graduate studies in theology and law. In the mid-sixteenth century, the first universities were created in Santo Domingo (1538), Mexico (1551), and Lima (1551). Later, those of Quito (1586), Bogotá (1594), Cuzco (1598), Chuquisaca (Sucre today, 1622), Guatemala (1681), Caracas (1721), Havana (1728), Santiago (Chile, 1738), and Guadalajara (Mexico, 1791) were established. The University of Córdoba (Argentina) was created in 1761, but legal studies there began later. These years are approximate because some historians define the founding date by the royal charter of foundation and others by the beginning of activity, generally a few years later (García Gallo, 1977, 1997; Rodríguez Cruz, 1973). In the case of Caracas, there was a law course a few years before the founding of the university (Leal, 1963; Pérez-Perdomo, 1981). In Bogotá most legal education took place in schools controlled by religious orders, not at the university (Uribe-Urán, 2000: 103–108). The policy of the

Spanish crown in the Indies, as the colonies in America were officially called, was to provide education to the colonists' male offspring in the main cities of the New World. Portugal did not create universities in Brazil, and the children of Brazilian colonists had to be educated in Coimbra.

Regardless of differences in the colonial policies of Spain and Portugal, all of Latin America was incorporated in the civil law tradition. They shared the tradition of a legal education offered by the universities, in which Roman and canon law studies had a central place. It is therefore instructive to analyze what was taught and what students learned, first in the Hispanic period and then when the countries achieved their independence. Additionally, an important question relates to the value or usefulness of those studies to the participants and their society at the time.

Even when Spanish policy allowed the education of a greater number of young men, growth in the student population was slow because *pureza de sangre* (blood purity) was an admission requirement. According to the statutes of the different universities, under *pureza de sangre* rules, only sons of "old" white Christians could be admitted as students (Leal, 1963). Women, Africans or those of African descent, Indigenous people or "sons of the earth," Moors, and converted Jews were excluded. With a small number of exceptions, recently immigrated white men were not eligible to pursue university studies. They were called *blancos de orilla* and were socially closer to the *pardos*, or free people of mixed blood, who performed manual trades.

Furthermore, university education was relatively expensive, not only because of the cost of tuition but also because it meant redirecting an important labor force within the family away from work. As a consequence, most students were young men from families that owned haciendas or plantations of some importance, or they were the sons of civil servants. They had in common that they could dedicate themselves to study while most young people were required to have productive employment from a very early age. These forces of social selection meant that universities consistently educated small numbers of students. In Caracas, at the end of eighteenth century, there were about fifty law students in any given year (Pérez-Perdomo, 1981:62). The population of Venezuela at that time is estimated to have been eight hundred thousand inhabitants. Caracas probably had a population of thirty thousand (Mago de Chópite, 1997), and other cities were smaller.

In practice, reflecting the changing times and the mixing of races that occurred in Spanish America, there were notable exceptions to these admission requirements, especially when families had wealth or the protection of high-ranking individuals (Uribe-Urán, 2000; Pérez-Perdomo, 2006). The rigid rules allowed, in fact, for exceptions. One of those exceptions was Antonio Rodríguez de León Pinelo (1595–1660), who was probably born in Valladolid, Spain, the son of conversos (converted Jews). He studied in San Marcos (Lima) and came to hold high positions in Spain, where he became rapporteur of the Council of the Indies. As a scholar, he was linked to the second Spanish Scholasticism and recognized as the author of the *Recopilación de las Leyes de Indias* of 1680, the voluminous compilation of Spanish legislation for the American kingdoms or colonies (Lewin, 1942). The family had the powerful protection of the bishop of Valladolid.

Another exception was Juan Germán Roscio, son of a *mestiza* and a Milanese of recent immigration. He studied theology and law at the University of Caracas, where he became the professor of civil (or Roman) law. Although his indigenous ancestry was evident in his appearance, he had the protection of the daughter of the count of San Javier. She herself was one of the most powerful women in Caracas in the second half of the eighteenth century. His admission to the Bar Association of Caracas faced serious obstacles because of the difficulties of proving blood purity. He was later very active in the independence movement, held high positions in the nascent republic, and wrote fundamental works. Among them was *El triunfo de la libertad sobre el despotismo* (1817), a major work of Latin American political thought of the independence period (Pérez-Perdomo, 2020). Roscio and León Pinelo are two well-known exceptions because they became important legal scholars, but they are far from the only exceptions.

Roscio left a record of his readings during different periods of his life and of the orientation of his teaching experiences, and so it is worth giving him special attention. His documented readings show him sharing the ideas of Spanish Catholic liberalism (Ugalde, 1992). He advocated equality, which was anathema to conservatives. At the same time, he was well versed in the Castilian and Indiano legislation and used them to support his views (Pérez-Perdomo, 2020).[12] He also serves us as a guide to legal education at the end of the eighteenth century. This is the report he presented on his teaching in 1803:

> The Constitution (of the university) imposes only the obligation to explain in this chair the four books of the Institutes of Justinian from three to four o'clock in the afternoon; but as here there is no other chair of Civil Juris-prudence, it is necessary to teach those subjects usually taught by the Prima and Vespers professors. We use the lights that the commentaries of Arnoldo Vinnio and Antonio Perez lend. This was the conduct observed in the re-gency of the aforementioned chair by my mentor and predecessor, the late Doctor Juan Francisco Zarate. He taught by himself what three professors do in other well-stocked and endowed universities. In addition to the teaching of the Pandecta, Instituta and Code, and without failing to comply with the Statute and assignment of his chair, he dictated and explained the Royal Law of Spain and the Indies, adding the legislation pertaining to the title, subject or paragraph of the daily reading. He included both the concor-dant ones and the contrary ones, modifying ones or derogatory ones. As a consequence of this, in literary acts or public disputes, he always proposed among the issues taken from the Instituta, some taken from the Partidas. Truly speaking, with the only investiture of Professor of Instituta, he also taught Prima, Vespers and Practical Law. This is a necessary knowledge for the people who are governed or judged by the Spanish rules that cannot be found in the Digests and Codes of the Roman Empire. I have constantly fol-lowed my mentor's footsteps since February 9, 1798, when due to his death, the Venerable Cloister did me the honor of entrusting me with the ownership of this Chair of Instituta. This is a chair that is in relation with other arts and sciences teaching for the better knowledge and help on civil matters. (García Chuecos, 1937:I,96, 97)

From Roscio's account, we can draw a number of conclusions re-garding legal education in this period. First, Roscio referred to a poorly endowed university, with only one professor of civil (Roman) law and one of canon law. According to his report, the professor was not limited to the explanation of the *Institutes* but also covered subjects such as the *Digest* that were taught in other courses in better-endowed universities.

In Prima they dealt with successions and matters relating to persons and in Vespers, with issues of possession and what today we call rights in rem. Another course, called *Digesto Viejo* (Old Digest), covered easements and procedural matters. For comparison, in Salamanca in the sixteenth century, there were four professors of Roman law, but only parts of the *Corpus Juris Civilis* were read, and they were selected for their relevance to the practice of law (Alonso Romero, 2012; Peset & Alonso Romero, 2018). Extrapolating from this, it is reasonable to infer that the sole professor of Roman law in Caracas was even more selective in the parts of the *Digest* and the *Partidas*, also a voluminous work, that were treated in class.

Second, the teaching method reflected the changes seen in Europe following the Middle Ages. Although the reading of the text was still fundamental, the teacher offered more explanations. This style is said to have begun with Alciatus (1492–1550), reputed to be one of the great early jurists of the *mos gallicus* (Monheit, 1997). The lecture method was very convenient for presenting the law in an organized way, something that cannot be achieved with a simple reading, or commented reading, of the *Digest* or even the *Institutes*. The medieval method does not allow for a systematic presentation of contents. In addition, if the professor wishes to incorporate other content, such as the Spanish law, the professor's lecture could readily serve to incorporate that information. This allows us to infer that, in addition to the commentated reading of the texts, lecture classes were offered, surely an innovation in the eighteenth century. On the other hand, "public disputes"—that is, the staging of the *questio*, were maintained.

Finally, the choice of Vinnius as a text shows the assimilation of contemporary thought in legal education in the colonies. The insistence on the teaching of *derecho patrio* (national law) was also one of the persistent themes of the enlightened thinking of the eighteenth century jurists (Alonso Romero, 2012; Coing, 1977). It is worth discussing whether democratic and liberal thought had also had an influence. Mijares (1953) detects the presence of Rousseau in Roscio's writing. Roscio's arguments for equality can be read as a resonance of Rousseau. Roscio may or may not have read Rousseau, but if he did, he did not quote him. Before 1810, Rousseau was forbidden reading in Spain and the colonies. To quote Rousseau, then, was not in Roscio's interest, as it would be interpreted as heterodox. Roscio was a liberal Catholic. His liberalism was well understood by Benito Juárez, who edited him twice in Mexico (Miliani, 1983). He was critical of the pope's political positions but remained a Catholic. The Venezuelan constitution of 1811, of which Roscio was a drafter, shows the influence of Locke, perhaps directly or through the Constitution of the United States of America, but the Venezuelan constitution of 1811 allowed public worship for Catholics only. The relationship with religion and the Catholic Church was one of the central problems for political thought in the nineteenth century throughout Spanish America (Aveledo Coll, 2011; Serrano, 2008). Roscio wanted to dissociate the Catholic Church from the conservative monarchy, but he was far from radical liberalism.

Thus, from the evidence of Roscio's experience, teaching was still focused on the Roman law as compiled by Justinian. In reality, however, all the elaboration of the law in medieval and modern Europe had transformed Roman law. Thanks to Vinnius, whose texts were the most widely used, students became familiar with Justinian's *Institutes*, but these were seen through the eyes of humanist jurisprudence and the school of natural law. The students also had some familiarity with the national legislation, especially with the *Siete Partidas*. In addition to Roman law, they studied canon law, which oriented them to Catholic theology and important texts regarding marriage and other sacraments regulating the status of persons. The texts were read in Latin, except for the *Siete Partidas*, which is in medieval Spanish. Given what we know of a teacher like Roscio, contemporary authors were probably not unknown, although they were not among the works discussed in class. Previous education was also important. Before entering into legal studies, students had courses in Latin, rhetoric, and grammar. Finally, to become lawyers, they had to complete an internship of varying duration depending on the time, and then the Audiencia, which was the highest court in the colonies, recognized them as lawyers. This recognition made them unpaid officials of the Crown, a high honor equivalent to a title of nobility (Uribe-Urán, 2000).

Roscio's writings demonstrate the scope and content of legal knowledge at that time. Obviously, the jurist had to handle Roman texts and Spanish legislation, but an educated jurist, such as Roscio, also displayed his knowledge of the Indiano legislation (rules for the governing of the

American colonies), historical erudition, and solid mastery of theology. In his lesser-known writings, such as those produced in his lawsuit concerning the Colegio de Abogados of Caracas (published only in Parra Márquez's 1952 history of this *colegio*), as in his best-known work (*El triunfo de la libertad sobre el despotismo*, 1817), Roscio handles with ease all bodies of knowledge. Law was thus a well-delineated, established body of knowledge and had connections with the other important fields of knowledge of the time. Law was an important intellectual discipline, and the lawyer was expected to be a scholar.

The previous analysis has also shown that legal education was not very different in the well-endowed universities and in universities with more modest means. The well-endowed ones could count on more professors who could certainly go more deeply into the readings, but the readings were the same as elsewhere. There was a common high legal culture in the Spanish world and perhaps in all of Europe: the European *ius commune*.

Popular culture was a different matter. In the eighteenth century, a large part of the colonial population was illiterate, which caused some significant difficulties. Those who studied law understood Latin ("God's language" at the time), comfortably used Latin expressions, and were familiar with the rules of political power. They could express themselves eloquently and argue convincingly. Toward the end of the eighteenth century, they were likely familiar with trends in contemporary political thought because forbidden books circulated in the colonies. Of course, the range and depth of knowledge depended on the intellectual strength of the individual. University law studies prepared those who studied not only for a job but also for a position at the top of the elite in the major cities of what is now Latin America. They were the *letrados*, or the lettered class, of the cities (Rama, 1984). They were generally members of, or connected to, the families that controlled agricultural production and large-scale commerce, the most important economic activities of the time. In short, they had a superior social position and culture. At the same time, though, the rules established by the Bourbon monarchy prohibited "sons of the country" from holding high government positions in the American colonies. This prevented local oligarchs from obtaining too much power but meant that, in practice, peninsular Spaniards held the positions (Burkholder & Chandler, 1977). This was one good reason most lawyers sided with independence or autonomy when the Spanish monarchy entered a crisis of legitimacy.

The high status of lawyers does contain within it a certain type of dysfunction. It was unthinkable for them to serve socially inferior clients. It was also improper or extremely uncomfortable for these potential clients to approach lawyers in a society with such pronounced social inequality. For these reasons, many of the usual activities of lawyers, such as drafting documents and providing assistance before courts or other public authorities, were carried out by people who were not university graduates and therefore not lawyers. To some extent, these *procuradores* and *tinterillos* replaced lawyers. The procurators were often impoverished white people (called *blancos de orilla*) who could write and knew the law to a varying degree. They were recognized by the *audiencias*. The *tinterillos* frequently were *pardos* (free mixed-race people) who knew how to write, advised in the shadows, and did not appear as signatories on any documents, so we know little about them (Becker, 2012). Although some of their functions were taken over by these individuals, lawyers in the new independent nations found politics to be an open field.

LAW SCHOOLS, LAWYERS, AND NATION BUILDING

The political importance of lawyers in the period from 1808 to 1830, corresponding respectively to the crisis of the Hispanic monarchies and the birth of the new Latin American states, has been documented in numerous studies (Gaitán Bohórquez, 2002; Pérez Collados & Rodrigues Barbosa, 2012; Pérez-Perdomo, 2006; Uribe-Urán, 2000). Lawyers continued to play important roles in these new nations throughout the nineteenth century, as Barman and Barman (1976) have shown for Brazil, Serrano (1994) for Chile, Gaitán Bohórquez (2002) for Colombia, and Pérez-Perdomo (1981) for Venezuela. They drafted a variety of documents; wrote constitutions, laws, and codes; and held high political office. One of their main tasks was to rethink the organization and functioning of law schools in universities. It was evident that these schools needed to train the new political elite and that the task of doing so could not be taken lightly.

Of course, how legal education should be improved and fulfill this important new role was controversial and gave rise to many conflicts. The discussion has been well documented for Brazil, where legal studies had to be created ex nihilo. The discussion took place in the Brazilian constituent congress (Câmara dos Deputados, 1977; Bastos, 1978; Falcão, 1978). The issue was also discussed in the constituent congress of Colombia (or Congress of Cúcuta of 1821), which determined that, in addition to basic education (Spanish and Latin grammar, philosophy, and mathematics), theology and law should be included. The government decreed (in the session of July 15) that curricula should be uniform throughout the country, and later, Vice President Santander identified "the authors whom young people should study" in the different chairs (Martínez Garnica, 2019:317–322). In Caracas, Bolívar was approached directly, and in 1827 he approved a special statute for the University of Caracas (renamed as Universidad Central de Venezuela) with a new curriculum (*Novísimos estatutos de la Universidad Central de Venezuela*, 1827). In other countries the discussion was perhaps less public, but in all of them, it was the political power that approved the curriculum and chose the texts for professors and students. These were concerns of high political relevance that could not be left to the judgment of professors alone.

In general terms, there was consensus on the direction of the law studies reform; the teaching of Roman and canon law was maintained, and constitutional law, national law, and international law were added. Political economy was also incorporated in Colombia, Brazil, Venezuela, and Chile, but not in Mexico. In several countries, natural law (Brazil, Mexico, Chile) and/or principles of universal law (Colombia, Venezuela, Mexico, and Chile) were also incorporated. The last two subjects were ideologically important. Whereas natural law referred to the concepts and rules developed by the school of natural law, the principles of universal legislation were a reference to the work of Jeremy Bentham. His works were translated into Spanish soon after their publication in English and became important and extraordinarily controversial. Their inclusion in the law curriculum generated heated conflict between liberals and conservatives (Pérez-Perdomo, 2006). The names of the courses did not always coincide with the subject matter we might expect. For example, at the University of Buenos Aires, created in 1823, the first professor of civil law, Pedro A. de Somellera, adjusted his lessons to Bentham's ideas and then published them in 1824, as *Principios de derecho civil* (Tau Anzoátegui, 1987:37).

The changes in the content of legal education were substantial and very much aimed at incorporating the most recent ideas, but they were in line with the Enlightenment project of the eighteenth century, which included greater attention to national legislation and rationalist ideas. The two tendencies clashed in the sense that Spanish legislation was considered disorganized, contained in compilations, and also originated by a repudiated political power. What was common at the time was criticism of Spanish legislation (Guzmán Brito, 1982:134–136; Tau Anzoátegui, 1987:23–26) and some distancing from Spanish authors. The alternative was the effort to develop national legislation along the lines of contemporary models. For the constitution, there was that of the United States of 1789, the French revolutionary constitutions, and the Spanish constitution of 1812, which was appreciated as liberal. Legislation, in accordance with the ideas of the time, was intended to be simple, clear, and limited (Pérez-Perdomo, 1988). However, the main model, which was the French Civil Code (1804), was tainted by its association with the French Revolution and Napoleon, neither of which was appreciated at all in Spanish America. To follow this model was controversial.

Instructional materials had to be chosen with extreme care because they needed to be carriers of "truth." European thought of the time was attractive, but it was tainted by Protestantism or Gallicanism and other heresies, and it could be subversive to the desired order. These books were no longer censored, or "punished" as Juan de Sala had put it, but they had to be adapted to the Catholic character of the new republics. Professors themselves had to make the necessary alterations to the text. Article 229 of the *Plan of Studies for the Republic of Colombia* explains their delicate mission thus:

> The authors designated in this decree for public teaching are not to be adopted blindly by the professors in all their parts. If one or some of them have doctrines contrary to religion, morality and public tranquility, or errors for any other reason, the professor must omit the teaching of such doctrines, suppressing the chapters that contain them and showing the students the errors of the author or authors on those points, so that they may beware of

them and in no way undermine the healthy principles in which young people should be imbued.

It was appreciated that the professor made omissions with discretion, a virtue applauded by the Governing Board of the Central University of Venezuela in the first professor of public law, Andrés Navarte, who was a professor between 1824 and 1828 (Leal, 1978).

Along similar lines, Andrés Bello opened his speech at the installation of the University of Chile on September 17, 1843, with a double profession of faith: to the lights of the new era and to morality and religion. "Morality (which I do not separate from religion) is the very life of society. . . . Those who imagine that there may be a secret antipathy between religion and the letters, slander one or the other." The task of professors was to emphasize the compatibility of enlightenment with religion and morality.

In general, the idea of "adapting" the ideas of the European Enlightenment to countries that were predominantly Catholic and in which there was no desire to antagonize the church, predominated until the mid-nineteenth century. The Catholic religion was considered not only part of national and personal identity and the supreme truth but also essential for the maintenance of social order. This thinking has often been called conservative when in fact it was both modernizing and moderately liberal on economic policy. It aimed to incorporate the new sciences, with the limitation that they could not be incompatible with revealed truth. In political and economic terms, it was moderate liberalism. It supported freedom of contract and trade and the protection of property, including the ownership of enslaved persons and the "dead hands" properties (given to a person or institution, generally the church and not available for sale). Obviously, liberalism was adopted with many limitations. It was conservative modernization, or more properly, moderate modernization.

Analyzing the texts that were chosen for teaching is quite revealing of the changing emphasis in legal education. For Roman law, which was essentially transformed into civil (private) law, some continued with the Vinnio, but Heineccius's *Antiquitatum romanorum jurisprudentiam ilustrantium sintagma* (1718), which was a systematization of the Roman rules, was considered an appropriate substitute for the new era. Another of

Heineccius's books was the favorite work for teaching natural law. *Elementa iuris natura et gentium* (1737) had already been adopted in Spain by the first professor of natural law in the Iberian Peninsula, Joaquín Marín y Mendoza, who published it in 1776, adding to the title *castigationibus ex catholicorum doctrina*. Today Heineccius is considered an imitator of the school of natural law who drew his ideas from Leibniz, Wolff, and other authors of the school, but in the late eighteenth and early nineteenth centuries, he enjoyed much greater prestige, and his work had broad diffusion in the Iberian world (Pérez Godoy, 2015). Andrés Bello translated and adapted his work on Roman law, making significant changes to it. Bello published it without the author's name, as it already differed from Heineccius's work; Bello did not put his own name as author (Hanisch Espíndola, 1981:77).

Emer de Vattel's *Le droit des gens et principes de la loi naturel* (1758) was the preferred text for teaching public international law. To help the students of Caracas, Francisco Javier Yanes partially translated this book in 1824, suppressing the sections that were problematic (Yanes, 1959). Years later, Andrés Bello, in the preface to his work *Principios de derecho de gentes* (1832), mentions Vattel as the canonical author but uses several other sources. In successive editions, Bello changed the title of the work to *Principles of International Law* and enriched it by elaborating ideas from many other sources. This work continued to be published throughout the nineteenth century in different Latin American countries and was a major contribution of Andrés Bello to the didactic literature in law. It also heavily influenced the practice of international relations and diplomacy in Latin America.

Benjamin Constant's *Course of Constitutional Politics* was the preferred textbook for constitutional law. Constant is still considered an important thinker of political liberalism. One of the difficulties is that his work refers to the parliamentary constitutional monarchy when the countries of Spanish America were organized as presidential republics. In the second half of the century, the work of Florentino González (1805–1875) replaced that of Constant in several Latin American countries. González was one of the intellectual leaders of Colombian liberalism (Mouchet, 1960). He taught in Chile, Argentina, and other countries, and his *Lecciones de derecho constitucional* (1871) was also used in other countries such as Venezuela. González's strategy was to concentrate on the explanation of the US constitution in order to analyze constitutional principles.

As may have become apparent, one of the major difficulties regarding the history of ideas in Latin America is the diversity of meanings attributed to the term "liberal." For the majority of the nineteenth century, "liberal" was synonymous with secular thinking and policies that would free citizens from the bonds of the Catholic Church and also allow the assets of the church to be introduced into the market. The church was the wealthiest institution; it owned much real estate and agricultural lands that could not be sold. Many liberal intellectuals and politicians supported the strengthening of the state, the only power that could serve as a counterweight to the Catholic Church. In most countries, secular liberals predominated at the end of the nineteenth century and adopted modern science, which at the time was connected to positivist and evolutionary thought. Frequently, these "liberals" were authoritarian, which also marked the transformations of law schools. However, "liberal" had other connotations. Those who advocated limiting the power of the state but considered the Catholic Church indispensable for maintaining order, and even respected its property rights, also called themselves liberals.[13]

Trazegnies (1979) asks why Latin America chose "second-rate" European authors, such as Heineccius, or later Ahrens and Pradier-Fodéré, for law school texts. His hypothesis is that their eclecticism made them appropriate for the conservative modernization that characterized Latin American legal thought in the early and mid-nineteenth century. Of course, the label "second-rate" is a difficult concept to evaluate. As for eclecticism, note that authors such as Bentham, Say, and Constant, who were not eclectic, were also adopted.

The field of legal education, which was the training ground for the political elite, was clearly rife with controversy. Law schools, and universities in general, were a showcase for the struggle for the predominance of certain ideas. For this reason, the occupation of professor was entangled in politics, and it entailed risks such as imprisonment, exile or replacement. A change in political alliances could have an important impact on a professor's life. The biographies of professors such as the aforementioned Florentino González or Ezequiel Rojas, both Colombians, the Argentine Dalmacio Vélez Sársfield, and the Venezuelans Cecilio Acosta and Felipe Larrazábal attest to the vicissitudes in the lives of some professors. Even in the twentieth century, university life in law schools was still very much affected by the political environment (Ortiz, 2015).

In the nineteenth century, professors and students were few. A chair had only one professor, and a professor also might have more than one chair. The professor was expected not to develop his own ideas but to disseminate the knowledge that was being produced in Europe, which was viewed as most advanced. The professor had to present and explain these ideas orally. Hence the lecture class became the main instrument of teaching. Because the teacher might also be a journalist, active in politics and working as a lawyer, he did not have time to write about what he taught (Pestalardo, 1914:88–91). Based on the evidence of the textbooks used and the occasional writings of the professors, Pestalardo was able to analyze in some detail the ideas held by each professor at the University of Buenos Aires. The situation in other Latin American countries was probably no different.

The controversial character of textbooks and professors derived from the fact that, at the time, ideas were perceived as either true or false, and the "true" ideas were the ones that needed to be taught. From the pedagogical point of view, the professor became a kind of preacher. There was no room for discussion, because truth was not negotiable. There was no room for opinions or divergent ideas. Hence, the lecture class was imposed as the appropriate method for teaching because it offered true knowledge in a well-organized form. The problematic or casuistic character of knowledge disappeared. The pedagogical advantages of disputes were still appreciated at the beginning of the nineteenth century, but they were soon replaced by examinations, which were initially solemn and public but later became more private. The requirement was for the student to be able to repeat back the professor's teaching. What we might call the side effects of lecture classes were also important. They taught obedience to authority and, given that the opinions of different professors might differ, practical skepticism (Pérez-Perdomo, 1975).

As the nineteenth century progressed, a new element was introduced. Each country in Latin America completed codifications of the law, and consequently, law courses increasingly focused on teaching and explaining the codes. It is generally accepted that codification nationalized and transformed law during the nineteenth century in Latin America (Guzmán Brito, 2000). Certainly, Roman law declined in importance, but that did not entail a major change in the content of teaching because, in general, Latin American codes were heavily influenced by the rationalized Roman law already taught in universities. In some countries, the courses were renamed according to the code that was to be taught. The educational method changed to reflect that new way of defining the law, as the professor read and explained the code article by article.

The French example was important at that time, and the commentaries on the codes were fully adopted as the standard legal writing. I have not found complaints in Latin America similar to those made by Flaubert in France, perhaps because of the availability of other courses, such as constitutional law, political economy, international law, and philosophy of law, which were more intellectually stimulating than the code-based teaching. In the twentieth century, some professors who continued with the exegetical method were negatively evaluated by their students. In contrast, in Argentina in the late nineteenth century, one finds a reference to the students' very favorable reaction to particularly eloquent lecture classes: "Ceballos was adored by his students who filled the classrooms, and the classes ended with ovations induced by the speaker's fiery words" (Scotti, 2015:152). In Venezuela, the stenographic version of Gil Fortoul's initial class of constitutional law in 1917 reports enthusiastic applause by the students (Gil Fortoul, 1956). The teaching of international, constitutional, or administrative law, more related to politics and less constrained by the codes, stimulated professors' eloquence.

UNIVERSITY REFORMS AND TWENTIETH-CENTURY TURBULENCE

In the late nineteenth and early twentieth century, a number of Latin American cities grew, and overall economic activity increased. An urban middle class started to expand. The pressure of economic and demographic changes was felt in the universities. The need for change in the law schools was especially pressing. This tension was particularly visible in Argentina, which had received a large influx of immigrants, had urbanized and industrialized, and had a thriving middle class. It had become one of the richest countries in the world. In Argentina, as elsewhere in Latin America, law schools were largely staffed by successful lawyers who were recruited to teach but who did not make university activities their center of attention (Colmo, 1915). University and public libraries and material facilities were poor, and as a consequence of these various factors, research and publications were minimal.[14]

As legal education became an issue, it also became an object of intellectual interest. The second decade of the twentieth century saw three important publications on legal education that reveal the intense interest in the subject in Argentina (Colmo, 1915; Martínez Paz, 1913; Pestalardo, 1914). Colmo's work is especially critical; it emphasizes that the existing system of legal education did not fulfill its practical-professional or scientific functions. It is interesting to note that the bibliographical commentary made by Lévêque (1918) pointed out the similarity between the Argentine curriculum and the French one, as well as the similar problems they produced.

Concern about the poor functioning of universities in Argentina led to the so-called Córdoba Reform in 1918. Tünnermann Barheim (1998) attributes the reform movement to the emergence of an urban middle class that aspired to enter the university and to achieve social advancement. Another factor was the desire to modernize and to bring the university into harmony with new ideas. Córdoba was an Argentine national university at the time still very much controlled by the clergy. The students generated a powerful movement and won many of their demands from a new government that was sympathetic to their cause. Basically, the students demanded that the university be autonomous from government and church control and that the university community elect its own authorities. Co-government implied both the presence of professors and students in the governing bodies and their participation in the election of the rector and deans. The students requested that professors be chosen through a competitive process rather than by government appointment and that they have "academic freedom," that is, autonomy in the choice of texts and in the content of teaching. Students also called for the creation of incentives for research. The reforms they called for spread relatively quickly throughout Latin America.

The twentieth century saw increased investments in universities and efforts to improve legal education. The reforms varied from country to country. In Argentina, research activity increased, especially in relation to doctoral studies, and thanks to a relatively strong publishing industry, there were ample opportunities for publication. Other countries undertook legislative reforms related to universities, but nowhere did the effort to isolate the university from the political regime have the anticipated effect (e.g., Ortiz, 2015). When governments perceived a challenge to their power emanating from the university, they generally intervened. Beyond the legislation and the issue of autonomy, academic freedom had a liberating effect on teaching itself. Governments ceased to mandate the textbooks, and professors were more inclined to update their knowledge. Some even became more independent with respect to European authors.

The academic level of students remained poor. Sabsay and Barrancos y Vedia (1958) pointed out that, until 1956, the University of Buenos Aires accepted students who had not completed secondary school but had technical studies. Enrollment also soared because it was free. The university enrolled 8,069 law students in 1956. In 1957, when a high school diploma was required, enrollment dropped to 3,686. The anomaly is that most of the students did not take any exams, and about 25 percent of those who did take the exams did not pass. In fact, actual law students constituted less than 25 percent of those enrolled, a problem that persists at other Argentinian universities (Lista & Brígido, 2002:70). Undoubtedly, universities had (and in some cases, continue to have) a function other than being strictly educational (Falcão, 1979, 1984).

In Venezuela, reform efforts began in the 1930s, even though the complete set of proposals of the Córdoba reform were not adopted there until 1958 (Febres Cordero, 1959). But even in the 1920s some teachers sought to foster innovation. In a testimonial collected by Pérez-Perdomo (1981), Rafael Pizani reported that the students had study and reading circles and that they read Colin and Capitant in the original French as a complement to the professor's classes, something that required great effort on their part because of their limited French.[15] Colin and Capitant's *Cours élémentaire de droit civil* had been published in 1916 and was considered quite innovative at the time. The students were probably aware of the publication because the professor cited the new literature in class. Soon after, the Spanish translation of such novel legal literature appeared, usually published in Madrid or Buenos Aires.

Similar reforms and investments in university education occurred elsewhere, and law schools were not left behind. In 1939, for example, the new headquarters of the Law School of the University of Chile was inaugurated, an "icon of 20th century modernity" (Araya Espinoza, 2018). In the 1950s, the massive university campuses (*ciudades universitarias*) of the National Autonomous University of Mexico and the Central University of Venezuela were built. Universities began to hire full-time professors, to invest in libraries, and to require professors to report their publications.

Another major factor in the twentieth-century reform of legal education was the substantial influence of European-trained professors, especially Spanish, Italian, and German émigrés as a consequence of the Spanish Civil War, the persecution of Jews, and World War II. Luis Jiménez de Asúa, Werner Goldschmidt, and Renato Treves took refuge in Argentina. In Mexico, Niceto Alcalá Zamora and Luis Recasens Siches had an important impact. Manuel García Pelayo, Roberto Goldschmidt, Joaquín Sánchez Covisa, and Antonio Moles Caubet went to Caracas. These are the names of academic giants, but many more European professors had remarkable productivity and influence in Latin America (Martin Frechilla, 2006; *Revista venezolana de legislación y jurisprudencia* 2017; on Mexico, see López Villaverde, 2021). The immigrant professors were hired by the universities, and lacking the possibility of practicing the profession, they devoted themselves entirely to academic activity. Young graduates or homegrown professors also began to dedicate all their efforts to academic activity. For example, this is the biographical trajectory of Héctor Fix-Zamudio, the great Mexican legal scholar, for whom working with Niceto Alcalá Zamora was inspiring and helped him decide to pursue the academic life (Pérez-Perdomo, 2012). Thus, émigrés gave great impetus to research. At the same time, Latin American universities began a policy of creating research institutes within universities and hiring full-time professors, which allowed the employment of an increasing number of young people. Research on law experienced a boom.

Also in the mid-twentieth century, some Latin American universities or governments began to offer scholarships for recent graduates to pursue graduate studies in Europe or the United States. These scholarship programs were generous in Venezuela in the 1960s and 1970s.

Law was not the discipline most favored with scholarships, nor were law graduates the most interested in the additional training, given that it might carry the obligation to work full-time for the university or the public sector, depending on the origin of the scholarship. Nevertheless, a number of new graduates and young professors were able to take advantage of the opportunities for study abroad, and many returned as full-time professors. Legal publications and journals flourished (Melich Orsini, 1976; Pérez-Perdomo, 2006).

While the universities were improving with both more up-to-date professors dedicated primarily to academic activity and better buildings and libraries, dissatisfaction and sharp critiques of legal education were increasing. The explanation for this paradox is not simple. One factor is that the student body had changed; it had become larger and more varied. The democratization of education brought many more students to law schools.[16] Work in court or as paralegals was no longer accessible to most students. Thus, informal practical training disappeared for most. Additionally, the advent of television had changed the reading and study habits among young people, and the informal groups for reading and intellectual conversation that complemented the cultural part of legal education largely disappeared. Not surprisingly, students did not feel that they were being prepared well for professional life.

Furthermore, while young professors were coming into contact with the best universities in the world, most of the teaching staff belonged to the old school. Even in the middle of the century and beyond, there were still exegetical professors who limited themselves to explaining and commenting on the articles of the code. Other, more modern professors offered lectures with good systematization of a branch of the law, but that was no longer considered sufficient.

The second half of the twentieth century was a time of severe criticism of legal education and conflicts in law schools over reform efforts. These efforts intensified in the final decades of that century and in the early decades of the twenty-first century. The internationalization of a small but growing part of the professorship, the rapid spread of new ideas, the transformations of the legal profession, and what has been referred to as globalization, all increased the pressure to restructure legal education. These more recent trends are discussed in the concluding chapter.

CHANGE AND TRADITION

Merryman defined legal tradition as "a set of deeply rooted, historically conditioned attitudes about the nature of law, about the role of law in society and polity, about the proper organization and operation of a legal system, and about the way law is or should be made, applied, studied, perfected, and taught. The legal tradition relates the legal system to the culture of which it is a partial expression. It puts the legal system into cultural perspective" (Merryman & Pérez-Perdomo, 2019:2). From this complex definition, let us retain the characteristics of "deeply rooted, historically conditioned attitudes," which implies continuity over time but not immutability. As the previous analysis has shown, there were important changes in legal education and the conception of law within the civil law tradition. These changes were part of broader change in society that also encompassed the economy and political systems. Within a legal tradition there are transformations, but these tend to develop relatively slowly, conditioned by the weight of tradition. History matters.

If we limit ourselves to antiquity, we can see that Cicero's legal education differed substantially from that offered in the time of Constantine or Justinian. In the early classic period, it was a rather informal apprenticeship in the house of the jurisconsult. In the fourth century there were schools and paid teachers. This shift implies institutionalization and organization. Of course, Roman society had become much more complex; politically, it had become an empire. The law in the classic period was seen as embedded in society and drawn out of social relationships by the jurisconsults. In the late empire the law was seen as more strongly linked to politics. Emperors such as Theodosius and later Justinian took on the task of organizing and, ultimately, promulgating the law. The work of the jurisconsults of the classic era did not disappear. It was incorporated into the body of the law, but the meaning of their work changed. Their reasoning was no longer the product of experience and social understanding; it was selected and compiled in a written text approved by the political power. Legal knowledge became bookish, although incidentally, books as we know them did not yet exist. There were only scrolls.

Can we say that social and material changes determine political changes, changes in law and the conception of law, and finally legal education? When we look at history in a more granular way, we do not see such linearity. The various changes are slow and recursive, generating conflicts and hesitations. They do not necessarily follow the order that seems reasonable to the theorist. Historians, like someone examining old photographs, can appreciate the frozen moment, but the complex multidimensional film eludes us. We cannot isolate each strand and determine its impact on the other strands constituting the complex skein of change.

The law taught in the Middle Ages was supposed to be fully expressed in the Roman texts compiled by Justinian and the canons compiled by Gratian, but the experience of the professors and certainly their political interests caused them to adjust their interpretation to a new social context. Formally, the law was detached from politics. The professors' duty was to discover the social order within, for which the Roman texts were considered the guide, but society had changed, and applying the rules expressed in the texts was not an easy task. When the city statutes and decisions of councils and popes were also incorporated, the guides became more complex, and interpreters had greater room to maneuver (Sbriccoli, 1969). The resulting plurality of interpretations introduced confusion.

The European jurists of the *via moderna* considered the variety of interpretations and opinions to be part of the prior dark ages. Their reaction was to "purify" the Roman law with the help of linguistics and the "geometrical reasoning," which Roman jurists had supposedly used. Centuries later, this change in the conception of the law produced the French codes and German "legal science." The codes reflected reason, as the political power understood and imposed it, and legal science represented reason itself, aided by history. We live in a postmodern era in which we no longer believe much in reason as expressed in the Enlightenment. Furthermore, we generally think that it is not a good idea to place the law in the hands of politicians, although no one denies that they bear responsibility for approving statutes. The educational methods invented by the modern professors (e.g., exegesis, teaching lectures, law handbooks) are questioned not only for their pedagogical shortcomings but also for being indebted to a conception of the law that most legal scholars of the twenty-first century no longer share (Jamin, 2011).

In summary, this analysis shows that the civil law tradition has not been immutable and that changes have occurred in relation to legal education that are related to historical and social changes and also to changes regarding the conception of the law itself. In the civil law tradition, the conception of the law that we simplistically call "legal positivism" began to be questioned at the beginning of the twentieth century, but it was only at the end of that century that the impact of that questioning was felt in legal education. Legal traditions are not impervious either. The next chapter deals with the common law tradition, with the aim of showing that in its birth and development, it has been very much in touch with the civil law tradition, although its legal education remained separate from the universities until the nineteenth century. Special attention will be given to the changes taking place in the United States and the explanation for why renewal in the common law occurred first in America.

II

Anglo-American Legal Education

TRADITION AND INNOVATION

This chapter constitutes a historical analysis of the transformations of legal education in England and the United States, two countries that are important representatives of the common law tradition. Comprehensive historical studies of legal education in a tradition spanning several centuries are rare. There are studies that analyze specific periods in a given country or specific institutions that have been or are important in the task of training legal professionals. The intent of this chapter is to use those sources to build a broader picture. The work thus relies on an extensive bibliography, including studies and testimonies that have so far been little referenced by other authors. I also aim to dispel frequent misunderstandings about legal education and to discuss some generally neglected issues regarding the social dimension of legal education, a dimension that particularly stands out in a comparative analysis, such as the one presented here.

ENGLAND: COMMON AND CIVIL LAWYERS

Around 1800 and during the decades that followed, one of the features that differentiated the common and civil law traditions was the different way of training legal professionals. In the common law tradition, the legal profession itself was in charge of educating new professional cohorts. In contrast, the education of legal professionals in the civil law tradition was the responsibility of the universities and, within those, of the professors. As we saw in the previous chapter, law was learned by studying the *Corpus Iuris Civilis*, the great Justinian compilation of Roman law reinterpreted over time by important scholars. For that reason, lawyers in this tradition are called "civil lawyers." But the distinction between the training of common and civil law professionals should be qualified: a university education, though not necessarily in law, was useful in becoming a common lawyer, and countries of the civil law tradition often required a period of practice under the supervision of a legal professional (Bogdan, 2013).

A misunderstanding that must be dispelled from the outset is that the common law is independent of Roman law and grew out of customs developed in England. In the Middle Ages, when the common law was born, customs were local and diverse. As its name indicates, the common law was a shared law for all England because it was imposed by the royal courts, whose main seat was in London. Its birth was influenced by jurists who knew Roman law; the founding works of the common law were written in Latin, as were many important documents.[1] Stein (1992) has emphasized the closeness of the common law to Roman law. French was also used, or at least a peculiar language derived from French known as "Law French" (Baker, 1998). A very important work for the common law (*Littleton's Treatise*) was written in French around 1481 and later translated into English in the sixteenth century.[2] The reference to the languages of law shows that Roman and French law influenced the emergence and development of the common law. Contract law and even theoretical works that attempted to give common law a more systematic organization have been read and commented on in England from the eighteenth century to the present (Swaminathan, 2019). This book argues that the differentiation between common law and civil law results from the different type of education required of those preparing to deal with the law and that common law never was a completely indigenous development of the legal system itself.

England, like other countries in Europe, had universities where both Roman and canon law were taught. From the end of the twelfth century, the University of Oxford had professorships in both laws (Stein, 1999).

Cambridge University followed a few years later. On the occasion of the religious reform, Henry VIII prohibited the teaching of canon law, but the teaching of Roman law has been maintained until the present. Thus, in England, common law, applied by the royal courts, and civil law, applied by the Court of Chancery, coexisted. Given the limited remedies that could be obtained in the royal courts, litigants could turn to the king, who very early on delegated to the lord chancellor (and later to the Court of Chancery) the task of deciding litigious cases. This court sought an appropriate solution using equity or Roman law. Maritime law cases were heard directly by the Court of Chancery. For that reason, England had both common lawyers and civil lawyers, and the latter had a monopoly on litigation in the Chancery.

The serious political conflict at the end of the seventeenth century led to the ascendance of Parliament over the king. The civil lawyers had supported the monarch, and the victorious Parliament punished them with the loss of their privilege to litigate in the Court of Chancery. This step led to a loss in the importance of civil lawyers, and eventually to their disappearance in England (Levack, 1973; Squibb, 1977). In the legal system, equity remedies were formally incorporated into the common law (Baker, 2019).

In England, the legal profession is divided into two branches. One of them has the exclusive right to litigation; its members are today called barristers. The other branch, initially considered minor, is that of solicitors. Traditionally, solicitors provided legal advice to individuals and produced legal documents for them. They generally came from a modest social background and had lower status than barristers. For example, when a solicitor visited a barrister in his home, he had to enter through the service door (Abel-Smith & Stevens, 1967:188). Litigation before the royal courts was the area of the barristers, but the relationship with the client had to be conducted through the solicitor. In the second half of the nineteenth century, both branches made an effort to establish demanding requirements for entry and to control professional ethics, all of which increased their social prestige. Both barristers and solicitors were educated through apprenticeship, but their education was separate. The rationale for this separation was that it was necessitated by the different competencies of their professional practice, but it undoubtedly can be largely attributed to their different social origins. Their associations or guilds are also separate. Solicitors have grown in number (they are much more numerous than barristers), and because they are advisers to business firms, their income has become more substantial (Burrage, 1996). Money has partially erased the social hierarchy among lawyers in recent times. This chapter focuses on the barristers.

The early steps in the development of common law education are not clear (see Brand in Langbein et al., 2009). We know of two didactic works that are central to the birth of common law and legal education in England. The first of these is known as *Glanvill*, written in Latin. A modern English edition refers to it as *The Treatise of the Laws and Customs of the Realm of England Commonly Called Glanvill*. It was probably written around 1188. The second, known as *Bracton*, also has a similar name (*De legibus et consuetudinibus Angliae*, or The laws and customs of England) and was probably written between 1220 and 1230. These books constituted the common law in the sense that they attended not so much to local customs, which were very diverse, as to the actions and procedures of the royal courts (Baker, 2007, 2019). The other important source of the common law in its early stage was the *Year Books*, which began to be published at the end of the thirteenth century and continued until 1535. They were not published by any official body but were a kind of chronicle of litigation. These chronicles were focused more on the arguments presented than on the ultimate decision. The authors are not known, and there were many authors over the years of the books' publication. The books' public consisted of legal apprentices and professionals.

Beginning sometime after the Norman Conquest, litigants in the royal court were called "serjeants-at-law." The education of the serjeants was by apprenticeship, although it does not seem that the apprentices were educationally linked to a specific serjeant. Attachment was more to a court, where an area (the crib) was provided for them. After deciding a case, judges could give explanations of their decision to the apprentices (called barristers) (Baker, 1984). The Order of Serjeants eventually disappeared, and the lawyers who could litigate in the royal courts came to be called "barristers." The top layer of barristers, the king's (or queen's) counsel, took the place of the serjeants at the top of the profession.

In brief, England has maintained the tradition of education by apprenticeship. A first change was that apprenticeship passed to the office (chamber) of the barrister (Dicey, 1883). In the sixteenth and seventeenth centuries, the Inns of Court played a very important educational role (Prest, 1967, 1972). More recently, and as part of the transformation of legal education in the common law in the second half of the twentieth century, law studies in universities have come to play an increasingly important role (Walker, 1993).

A very important institution in English legal education was the Inns of Court in London. The translation for this institution would be a bar association but with several additional functions. The four inns were also houses where members could stay, where meals were served, and where various social and educational activities took place.[3] For about two centuries, ending with the serious political conflicts of the mid-seventeenth century, the inns sponsored formal educational functions such as lectures and mock trials, but this declined in the late seventeenth century and recovered only in the early twentieth century. In their heyday, they were regarded as the third university—the other two being Oxford and Cambridge (Morley, 1975; Prest, 1967, 1972). The inns were attended by young men seeking an education that included law and also other subjects. It was not necessarily education for professional practice. However, to be accepted as a barrister, young men had to eat a number of meals at the inn of attachment, which also maintained some control over the behavior of the applicant and of the members. The number of meals is a tradition that continues to this day (Baker, 2007, 2012).

The function of Inns of Court has not always been understood by comparative scholars. David (1965:40) regards them as barristers' clubs, for that is how they appear on the surface, but to view them simply as clubs neglects the important functions they performed of building professional identity and exercising discipline. The Inns of Court hold examinations for barristers' certification (equivalent to admission to the bar). They also highlight the varied functions of a legal education, one of which is the acquisition of language, concepts and principles, and an understanding of the structure of the law. Another is developing the skills or abilities needed to perform professionally, including learning to reason or think like a lawyer. A third, and no less important, function is socialization in the profession: knowing how to recognize and deal with other members of the profession, communicating effectively with them, and observing their codes of conduct. The Inns of Court serve this third function very well. The apprenticeship in the barrister's office fulfills the second. The first was acquired by reading the books considered important to the profession. Traditionally this was less formalized in England than in the rest of Europe, but the importance of particular books in shaping an idea of law and legal language is probably as relevant in the common law as in the civil law tradition.

This description omits aspects of general training. The expectation was one of social self-selection reinforced by the cost of education; only upper-class men could aspire to become barristers. As a consequence, prior general education was ensured, as was, more generally, barristers' satisfaction with their own training. The relative democratization of English society after World War II led to a questioning of the system and acceptance of the idea of a university education for the legal professions. Certainly, universities are much more efficient and systematic in transmitting the conceptual foundation of legal practice. The Inns of Court or apprenticeship experience is weak in this regard but strong in the socializing dimension of the profession.

One aspect of the formation of the common law that is usually not emphasized is the importance of certain books that were intended to be instructional. *Glanvill, Bracton*, and, later, the *Year Books* were written for apprentices and at the same time helped to constitute the common law. They implied a configuration of legal knowledge, although it was far from being a systematic arrangement. In the sixteenth century, the *Year Books* declined and were replaced by books with a thematic arrangement called abridgments. Perhaps the most famous of these was that of Fitzherbert, published around 1514, which organized the material topically and, in a way, replaced the *Year Books*. A few years earlier the first treatise had appeared, which was *Littleton's Treatise on Tenures* (possession), one of the first books printed in England. Translated into English and annotated by Coke, it became the most frequently published law book in the history of the common law (Baker, 2019).[4] Thus, like civil law, the common law is also a bookish knowledge; the books were different from those of the civil law tradition but were influenced by it.

In summary, between the eighteenth and the mid-twentieth centuries, legal education in England and on the European continent differed fundamentally. In continental Europe, legal education was the task of the universities, and consequently, universities regulated entry into the profession. A court accepted the person as a lawyer, but that was only a formality. In England, the practitioners themselves were responsible for legal training, and it was the organized profession that admitted new members. Naturally, this implied different training. What professionals could provide was the apprenticeship in a trade, that is, the opportunity to practice it under the supervision and advice of a more experienced barrister (or solicitor, as the case may be) (Morley, 1975). In contrast, the training of the legal profession in continental Europe and Latin America was in the hands of the universities and their professors and had a greater claim to scientific status.

The foregoing description is general and has not accounted for the efforts of leading English jurists to change legal education and give universities a greater role. The Law Society was generally inclined toward such projects, but the Inns of Court blocked them. As a result, English universities developed teaching in areas such as philosophy of law, comparative law, history of law, international law, and criminology, but preparation useful for the practice of law remained in the hands of the profession (Abel-Smith & Stevens, 1967:165–180). One possible explanation is conservatism, but the roots are likely also social. Barristers came from the English upper class. Requiring university legal education would mix aspiring barristers with aspiring solicitors, blurring the status differences between them. Furthermore, barristers generally looked down on professors as socially inferior. Thus, the English social structure was likely the main obstacle to strengthening the university role in legal education.

Nevertheless, the efforts of universities and professors are instructive. In 1753, William Blackstone began teaching English law at Oxford, and in 1755, the Vinerian Professorship in English Law was established.[5] Blackstone's lectures gave rise to *Commentaries on the Laws of England* (1765), which was enormously influential, although more so in the American colonies and later in the United States, than in England. Oxford made further efforts in the second half of the nineteenth century and created a law school with notable professors in philosophy of law and international law but little success in attracting students (Lawson, 1968).

Blackstone taught until 1766, and his successors certainly did not have his intellectual brilliance. This changed in 1882, when Albert V. Dicey (1835–1922) was appointed. Dicey had been educated at Oxford and had a very distinguished career in London as a barrister beginning in 1863 (Hanbury, 1958). His first lectures as a Vinerian professor were published and became a fundamental work on constitutional law (*Introduction to the Study of the Law of the Constitution*, 1885). He also published an important work on private international law (*Conflict of Laws*, 1896). Dicey wrote two works of interest on legal education. In his inaugural lecture on English law, Dicey asks whether English law could be taught in universities (Dicey, 1883). His lecture analyzed in detail how apprenticeship operated, drawing from his own experience. In the barrister's office (chamber), the apprentice was given a written summary of an actual case, which might bear no relation to the readings he had done on law. His task was to prepare a draft of a legal argument related to the case that was arbitrarily assigned to him. He received very little help from the lawyer, who was usually too involved in his own business to pay attention to the trainee. Generally, the experience was disorienting for the trainee. Dicey concluded that college is the appropriate place to learn law. Years later he visited Harvard Law School and described in detail the teaching there in an article that will be discussed later (Dicey, 1900).

In the second half of the twentieth century, England witnessed important changes, which can be only summarized here. There was continued resistance to change. One factor contributing to this resistance, identified by Twining (1967:425), was that consideration of the experience of other countries was seen as unpatriotic. Major reform occurred in only one respect: universities became more important in the preparation of lawyers in the late twentieth century. In 1970, 80 percent of new admissions as barristers and 40 percent of those admitted as solicitors were university graduates, though not necessarily in law (Morley, 1975:368). Beginning in 1990, undergraduate studies in law became virtually mandatory (Walker, 1993). In short, even though the profession controls entry through examinations and requires internships and meals at the Inns of Court, university legal studies have become a requirement for examination registration. English law firms have internationalized, and foreign lawyers constitute a significant presence in London. Universities have been a more welcoming environment regarding internationalization than have the Inns of Court and the Law Society (Platsas & Marrani, 2016). Furthermore, the legal education that developed in the United States had a major influence on the transformation of English law schools from 1970 onward.

THE UNITED STATES: THE BEGINNINGS

English colonization in America began a century after Spanish colonization did, and the English colonies were extremely poor for a relatively long period (Elliott, 2006). Because the colonizers carried ideas and experiences with them, they transferred ideas of the law and of rights to the new colonies just as they did their language. The new society was much simpler than English society was, and therefore, institutions and rules were simplified or adapted to the social circumstances of the colonized territories (Friedman, 1973). Institutions such as the jury were passed on without much modification, but this was not the case with the institutions of legal education and the legal profession, which were more specifically connected with English social structure. The distinction between barrister and solicitor and organizations similar to the Inns of Court were not transplanted, probably because of the more socially democratic character of the colonies resulting from the absence of an aristocracy and wide availability of land ownership (Hurst, 1950:252–276).

In the seventeenth century, a small number of barristers and solicitors came to America, but they generally did not find society very welcoming. In the following century, as the economy became more complex, society grew more receptive to lawyers, and some lawyers who were born in this part of the world, especially in Virginia and South Carolina, received their training in England. The first of these was Benjamin Lynde, who was admitted to the Middle Temple (one of the Inns of Court) in 1692 and later returned to Massachusetts (Stoebuck, 1968). Apart from the option of going to London and training there, which was available to few people, an aspiring lawyer had three options: to study on his own, to serve as a clerk or assistant in a court or government office, or to serve as an apprentice to an established lawyer (Moline, 2002:779). Each colony had its own regulations that later influenced the development of organizational structures of the profession (Chroust, 1965). Hurst (1950) suggests that until the mid-eighteenth century, most lawyers were individuals who could express themselves well orally and in writing but lacked any real professional training.

Nevertheless, by the end of the eighteenth century, there were a number of well-trained lawyers, and both independent law schools and university law schools were founded. These institutions offered classes on the law but no curriculum for training as a legal professional. The first professor of law was George Wythe, first appointed to the Board of Visitors of the College of William and Mary in Virginia in 1761, and in 1779 to the new Chair of Law and Police. Among his early students were Thomas Jefferson (later president of the United States) and John Marshall (later chief justice of the US Supreme Court). Legal studies did not attract many students and were perceived as part of general studies or as preparation for civic life. As in other professions, it was believed that the law had to be learned in practice (Friedman, 1973:81–88; Warren, 1912:341; Reed, 1928). In university courses, the professor explained the law, but one did not learn how to be a lawyer. Jefferson's education is a good example of the importance of apprenticeship. Wythe, his professor, was also an eminent lawyer, and Jefferson went to work with him as an apprentice. Wythe introduced Jefferson to the great law books and initiated him into legal practice (Bernstein, 2004; Konig, 2012). A legal education in the same style can be seen in John Adams, another of the founding fathers of the United States (Ferling, 1993).

In the early years of the independent life of the United States, Columbia University was especially distinguished by the presence of its first professor of law, James Kent (1763–1847). His biography shows the type of education that a jurist-intellectual received at the time. He was a student at Yale, and in accordance with tradition, he was placed by his father as an apprentice to Egbert Benson, a prestigious New York lawyer and later New York State attorney general. Kent carefully read Grotius and Pufendorf; books on the history of England, including Hume; and a history of the common law. Already accepted as a lawyer, he continued his education in Latin, Greek, and French, and he read the classics (Goebel,

1955:6). He was a professor at Columbia for two terms, in 1794–1798 and 1821–1826. Kent lectured to students as his main teaching method. Between 1826 and 1830, he published his *Commentaries on American Law*, one of the most important legal works of the nineteenth century in the United States. It consists of six parts (in four volumes), covering international law, US government and constitutional jurisprudence, the law of the several states, the law of persons, personal property, and real property. From his papers, we can see that his teaching was quite comprehensive in different areas of law. The emphasis on property and absence of treatment, at least directly, of contracts and tort law, which would later become the focus of legal studies, is striking. Kent's commentaries became a work much appreciated by those studying law (Goebel, 1955:23–25).

Without institutional frameworks, the scope and quality of legal education by apprenticeship depended very much on the character and disposition of the lawyer/master. Testimonies collected in Warren (1912) suggest that such education was basically independent reading of works such as Coke's or Blackstone's, without further explanation by the lawyer, as well as what was learned by transcribing documents in an era when everything was handwritten. Some independent law schools offered a practical education that had the advantage over law offices of not subjecting students to the menial tasks of paralegals (Hurst, 1950). Several lawyers distinguished themselves by their dedication to their apprentices and their interest in having them learn law. This gave rise to the so-called proprietors' schools, which were educational institutions that emerged as an extension of a lawyer's office. These schools were not constituted in the formal sense that we know today. They did not issue a diploma or certificate, but they provided a letter certifying that the person had studied ("read") law for a certain period of time, and that training was valid as an apprenticeship period in order to qualify as a lawyer. Some of these schools achieved remarkable development. The most successful was that of Lichtfield, which had fifty-three students by 1813. In its half century of operation (1780s to 1830s), it trained a thousand lawyers, an average of twenty per year (Langbein, 2004a, 2004b; McKenna, 1986).

Because professional qualification was granted by a judge who confirmed that the candidate had good training and reputation, different models of legal training were possible, including these proprietors' schools. The requirement was a period of apprenticeship of several years, but it was considered an asset, at least in major urban areas, if the candidate had a university education. In more rural areas, where fewer lawyers were available, the requirements were lower. Twelve of the thirteen colonies that initially formed the United States had an apprenticeship requirement by 1780 (Stevens, 1983:3). Independence and the radical way in which laissez-faire principles were understood caused the requirements to weaken, and by the middle of the nineteenth century, apprenticeship was no longer generally required. In 1800, fourteen of the nineteen jurisdictions still required an apprenticeship. In 1840, eleven of thirty required apprenticeships, and in 1860, nine of thirty-nine (Stevens, 1983:7).

Despite the weakening of the requirements for legal apprenticeship, lawyers maintained social prestige. They brought to court the conflicts that arose in a newly independent country, and the judges, who in the common law tradition are seen as part of the same guild and independent of the government, made very important decisions in shaping the new society. A keen observer like Tocqueville (1835–1840) noted early on the importance of judges and lawyers in US society. He observed that they occupied the social place that corresponded to that held by aristocrats in Europe and that they were central to both the government and the social life of this new democracy. Indeed, in a society without the class distinctions that existed in Europe, lawyers had social prestige and the intellectual formation that enabled them to hold positions of the highest rank in politics and business.[6] They were part of the rapid expansion of society in the first half of the nineteenth century and beyond. Hurst (1956) pointed out the creativity of lawyers and judges in unleashing the energy of nascent capitalism. Gilmore (1977) called the era the "age of discovery." It was certainly a time of enormous economic and demographic expansion, and the number of lawyers also grew rapidly as the population expanded. In 1850 there were 23,939 lawyers; in 1860, 34,839 (Reed, 1921:442; Stevens, 1983:22). The relative figure (lawyers per 100,000 population), was fairly stable: 103 in 1850, and 105 in 1870.

A window on legal education in the United States around the middle of the nineteenth century is available thanks to a long letter from the Swiss-American jurist Georges-Auguste Matile to the French professor

Édouard Laboulaye, who published it in Paris (Matile, 1864). Matile (1807–1881) was born in Neuchâtel, Switzerland, and studied law in Heidelberg and Berlin, where he was a student of Savigny. He obtained his doctorate in 1829 and had a distinguished career in Neuchâtel. He taught law, held a number of high political offices, and wrote on the importance of the local customs versus Roman law in the history of Neuchâtel. A political revolt forced him to emigrate in 1849, and he left for the United States. There he taught at Princeton and in Philadelphia, where he was admitted to the bar. In 1856, he acquired US citizenship and took a position as librarian in the US Patent Office in Washington, DC. He associated with the intellectual elite and contributed articles to the local newspapers (Gigandel, 1991).[7]

Broadly speaking, his letter laments the sad state of university legal education in the early 1860s. Matile (1864:6) wrote that the general idea in the United States, as in England, was that law was a trade learned by reading relevant books and working in the office of a lawyer, for whom the apprentice ran errands and wrote documents. Law was not considered a science. There were no legal journals, and the libraries were very poor. He recounted an incident in which he arrived at the library of an important institution and found the librarian absolutely baffled by his request to see the *Corpus Iuris Civilis*. This anecdote is important in two respects. It reveals not only the poverty of law libraries in the United States at the time but also the fact that a continental European jurist considered the *Corpus Iuris* a fundamental, practical book that should be available in any library with law books. Matile reported the limitations of Harvard's law library despite considering it one of the best in the country.

Matile (1864:5) was concerned that university education was not the province of the federal government and that the states were not concerned with it except to formally recognize the initiative of citizens in establishing a school. He also complained about the difficulty of obtaining data about legal education, but Matile had an investigative spirit. Using various sources, he traced a panorama of legal education, both schools that were part of universities and independent ones. He identified eighteen law schools with a total of 1,002 students, or an average of 56 students each (Matile, 1864:11). The population of the United States at the time was thirty-five million.

Matile also observed that each university operated in its own way, and there was no significant relationship between them, even if they were neighbors. The state showed no interest in legal education, and the schools had few resources. Harvard was one of the most important schools, and it had ninety students and three law professors. Matile wrote: "I could cite only one school that has four professors; the others have only three, two, and even one. Often one observes that a school opens only to close soon after, due to the absence of a teacher or students" (1864:3).

At the time of Matile's writing, the most reputable law school was Columbia, which in 1857 established a general curriculum that included constitutional law, comparative law, natural and personal law, Roman law, and political economy (Gordon, 2007:343). Columbia's reputation was due in large part to the dynamism of Professor Theodore Dwight, who arrived at Columbia in 1858 and taught there until 1891 (Stevens, 1983:23). The professorial lecture was the main method of teaching; the lectures followed Blackstone's outline, though with more emphasis on commercial law. Students also read Kent's work. In addition, there were optional debating societies and moot courts (Friedman, 1973:239).

The length of study in the schools analyzed by Matile varied from six months to two years. Most of the schools did not administer examinations, and after their short stay, students could register as lawyers. Those who had not studied law could become lawyers by taking an examination (Matile, 1864:7). Despite the deficiencies of law schools, the education they provided was superior to that obtained by apprenticeship. This was noted by Abraham Lincoln, who, as a well-known lawyer in Illinois during 1855, considered studying law at a university so that he would be prepared when university-educated lawyers arrived in the newer western states (in Stevens, 1983:19).

Compared with historical research that has made use of various archives, the data that Matile obtained were incomplete, but they were good approximations. Archival data show that by 1840, there were nine law schools affiliated with universities, with a total of 345 students (Stevens, 1983:8). By 1860, there were twenty-one law schools and an estimated 1,400 students (Stevens, 1983:21). Most of the schools were not attached to universities. At that time, lawyers numbered 34,839, meaning that only a small percentage had attended a law school. The apprenticeship requirement had declined as the number of schools increased. In 1860, only nine of thirty-nine jurisdictions required it (Stevens, 1983:7).

Despite the defects he identified in professional training, Matile noted that there were a number of very capable judges and lawyers, and above all, the common people seemed satisfied with the lawyers and judges they had. He attributed the adequate preparation of the best lawyers to their natural intelligence, to the practical and commonsense foundation of American education, to the widespread embrace of liberty, and to the active political life of the country (Matile, 1864:14). Overall, however, Matile found the situation unsatisfactory and feared that the recognition of the scientific nature of law and development of better professional preparation would be delayed, but he counted on the general dynamism of American society for a light note of optimism. In general, it seems that Matile's concerns and relative optimism were justified. The improvements began a few years after the publication of his letter and were initiated at Harvard.

HARVARD AND LEGAL EDUCATION IN UNIVERSITIES

A note published by Harvard's law school professors in 1870 shows the deplorable state of legal education and the beginning of innovation at Harvard ("Harvard Law School," *American Law Review* 5, no. 1, 1870).

> For a long period of time, the condition of Harvard Law School has been almost a disgrace to Massachusetts. We say "almost a disgrace" because undoubtedly several of its courses were good, and no law school can be considered hopelessly bad. However, a law school awarding degrees without having tested students was causing injury to the profession and discouraging real students. Possession of a diploma meant nothing except a period of residence in Cambridge or Boston. Just as in England a number of meals entitles one to be part of the bar, so a number of months' residence at Cambridge authorized the degree of Bachelor of Laws . . . We are pleased to learn that the old system has been abandoned. A circular issued by the Faculty states that the LL.B. degree will only be conferred on students who pass examinations in all required courses and at least seven elective courses, after having been in school for at least one year.

In practice, the purpose of the circular was to require students to spend two years in school. In the first year, they had to pass the required courses, and in the second year, the elective courses. Subsequently, a third year was added, which is still required in most US law schools today.

The changes that occurred in the last third of the nineteenth century were general across all universities. Until the middle of the century, universities were perceived as institutions where one could acquire general culture, especially in the classical humanities. A group of scholars and entrepreneurs perceived that universities could play an important role in the teaching and development of scientific disciplines (Mattingly, 2017; Touraine, 1974). One of these innovators was Charles William Eliot, member of a prominent Boston family and a professor of chemistry with an interest in educational systems. For two years, Eliot traveled in Europe and studied the organization and functioning of universities in Germany and France and their relationship to scientific and economic development. His articles on university reform attracted attention, and he was appointed president of Harvard College in 1869. His leadership and forty-year presidency helped transform a provincial university into one of the most important in the world (Hawkins, 1972). Eliot appointed Christopher Columbus Langdell dean of Harvard Law School and gave him the task of strengthening the scientific underpinnings of legal education.

With Eliot's unconditional support, Langdell pushed a risky reform plan that was based largely on Eliot's ideas (Chase, 1979). Langdell set out to distinguish law as a science from the practice of law. One aspect of these reforms was the plan to convert law studies into graduate-level studies. He instituted the requirement of examinations to pass courses, and the examinations were to be anonymized to avoid favoritism. The library was transformed into a resource for research, and teaching became a professionalized career. For that reason, professors should not be lawyers who practice law but instead should be devoted to scientific and university activity (Feldman, 2004; Schlegel, 1985).

The science of law, according to Langdell, consists of carefully analyzing cases to discover their axiomatic principles and then applying those principles with rigorous deductive logic. Thus, there is a legally (or logically) correct solution for each case. The science of law, in this perspective, is normative. It tells practitioners how they should reason and thus can prevent or correct miscarriages of justice. Langdell set out to create a scientific method from the primary materials of law. The idea was to extract and understand the principles that determined decisions. To teach scientific methodology requires that the student conduct the experiment, not just watch the teacher do it. In law, a laboratory where students work with chemicals, plants, or tissues is not possible. Rather, the fundamental equipment is the library, and the primary materials, according to Langdell, are the opinions of senior judges, conveniently edited so that students can perceive the thread of reasoning and grasp the principles that the judge applied (or failed to apply). The classroom is the laboratory. The professor's job is to help the student understand the case and discover the principles in the judge's reasoning through properly formulated questions (Langdell, 1887).

This model led to Harvard's most important contribution to legal education, the method generally called the "case method" or the "Socratic method" (Stevens, 1983:51–72ff.). Case analysis was not Langdell's invention, but his innovation was focusing the class on the students, pushing them to discover the principles that allow for the correct resolution of the case. Langdell's method does not focus on the study of precedent, because judges' decisions can be criticized if those judges have misapplied the principles that allow for the correct resolution of the case. Nor does it focus on teaching the rules of law; rather, it focuses on analysis and reasoning, using the proper legal language. James Ames wrote about the role of the professor in this teaching method (Ames, 1913). When he was appointed a professor, Ames was a recent graduate with an interest in teaching who especially distinguished himself in the use of the case method. In practice, the case method also encouraged competition among students and stimulated a kind of Darwinian selection.

Langdell thus became the chief architect of the modern American law school, although Chase (1979) gives more credit to Eliot. Langdell's ideas and reform efforts have given rise to a very extensive bibliography analyzing his thought and work (Kimball, 2004, 2009). It is claimed that his thought was influenced by the formalist positivism of John Austin, a very important philosopher of law in the second half of the nineteenth century, although the educational ideas came more from Pestalozzi, as interpreted by Eliot (Chase, 1979). The ambition to achieve a science of law independent of morality and of the political and social aspects that interfere with its exercise was widely shared at the time. Langdell rejected legislation as an object of study, given that legislation was heavily tinged with political choices that he disliked and was not a foundation on which science could be built. Hence, the fundamental subjects were those of private law (contracts, property, tort, and procedure). The idea was also to concentrate on relatively few cases from which he chose to extract principles. For Langdell, law had a place in the university only if it was indeed a science and not a pure practice (Langdell, 1887).

The initial reaction was one of rejection. Harvard Law School lost students, and the method (referred to as "Mr. Langdell's method") was considered "abominable" by some people (Kimball, 2006, 2009). Justice Oliver Wendell Holmes, commenting on his work, called Langdell a "theologian of law" (Holmes, 1880; Levine, 1993). Harvard stayed the course, though, and within a few years, it became a benchmark of excellence in legal education (Coquillette & Kimball, 2015). However, the overall transformation of legal education was slow. At the beginning of the twentieth century, Ernest W. Huffcut (1902) presented a report to the American Bar Association on progress made in the previous decade (1890–1900). He found that in 1901, there were ninety-eight programs offering legal education and more than fourteen thousand enrolled students. Within the decade, the number of law students per one hundred thousand people had more than doubled, from 7.2 to 16.6 (Huffcut, 1902:404). The problem was quality. Most of the programs were proprietary schools that appeared and then disappeared just as quickly. They awarded degrees without the individual having received any instruction (Huffcut, 1902:405). In terms of admission, forty-three schools had no entrance requirements, forty-four required a high school diploma, three allowed advancement in the law school while pursuing an undergraduate degree, and only four required an undergraduate degree and three years of study.

Huffcut's report also addressed the issue of educational methods. "(T)he law school world is still in some ferment over the system introduced by Professor Langdell more than thirty years ago. It is plain, however, that that method has made great headway . . ." (Huffcut, 1902:408). He found that in law schools that were part of a university or had an endowment of their own, twelve schools were using the case and casebook system, and thirty-four were still using the professor's textbook and lecture system.

Clearly lecture classes and textbooks still dominated in 1901. These law schools showed some improvement in their resources, particularly in terms of their libraries. In 1894, only six schools had libraries exceeding five thousand volumes. By 1901, twenty-five schools exceeded that figure, and three exceeded thirty thousand (Huffcut, 1902:408). Huffcut also noted that the number of full-time faculty was increasing substantially, although he provided no figures. Practicing lawyers and judges were called only for specific courses in these law schools.

An important testimony of what a Harvard class was like around 1900 is found in Dicey's article (1900). As noted earlier, Dicey was the Vinerian Professor at Oxford, and in keeping with tradition, he taught with lectures that were the basis of his published works. He visited Harvard and gave a fairly detailed description of the education being provided and an analysis of the work of the major professors. He observed a class of James Ames and offered this description:

> From the first moment (the professor) joins the class he has placed in his hands the huge collection of contract cases edited by Langdell. The cases are placed under different heads, as for example, under "Offer and Acceptance," and under each head are arranged in historical order. Our student is neither assisted nor confused by printed comments. He is left without the aid even of head-notes. . . . He must, if he can, see their point. . . . He then comes with 100 or 200 companions to the lecture. Professor Ames has the names of the students before him. He calls now upon one, now upon another, to state the result of a definite case. He asks questions about it; he raises every point that the case contains; he suggests, in the way of questions, variations on the case; he states in the form of observation, its real gist. . . . The discussion was unforgettable. It was perfectly orderly; it was filled with animation. The principle involved was impressed upon me as it never had been before. (Dicey, 1900:56–57)

Dicey compared the method with others that were prevalent in England. The fact that the student had to exert himself in an unfamiliar field and get oriented by himself seemed similar to the effort of the apprentice when the barrister asked him to prepare the draft of a report. He compared the lively discussions it generated among the students to the discussions of philosophical texts that occurred at Oxford. He felt that the method produced much deeper learning than did lectures.

There were other activities in law schools that complemented formal learning: the legal clubs and moot courts (mock trials), which train for forensic argumentation, and work on the school's law review, which trains for research.[8] He also emphasized the catechetical nature of training at Harvard.

Dicey also noted the context of US legal education. Unlike in England, in the United States, the legal profession is unified; that is, it recognizes a single category of lawyer, and law is practiced in firms. The young graduates were hired by law firms as soon as they finished the school. Thus, they had a job and an ensured income from the start, which was not the case in England. The elite law school and the law firm were thus complementary. He also emphasized the difference in the purpose of legal education. At Oxford, legal education was meant to be formative, whereas it was more scientific-professional at Harvard. Thus, Oxford gave importance to subjects such as philosophy of law, international law, and Roman law. These subjects had no place at Harvard because they were not viewed as part of the science of law or advancing the students' professional training (Dicey, 1900).

PERSISTENCE, CRITICISM, AND TRANSFORMATION

The so-called Harvard model took some fifty years to spread, but it eventually caught on, and by 1925, it dominated legal education throughout the United States (Coquillette & Kimball, 2015; Friedman, 2002:33–39ff.; Kimball, 2021). This expansion of the model is all the more remarkable because there is no ministry or board to guide or control higher education in the United States. The influence of the American Bar Association, created in 1878 and controlled by elite lawyers, has been highlighted as an important factor in this success. The interest of these lawyers was to enhance the social prestige of the profession and to establish high ethical standards for the practice of law. They also were interested in legal education and soon formed a special committee that gave rise in 1900 to the Association of American Law Schools. In 1905, this association called on its members to support the requirement of a high school diploma for admission to law school and for legal studies to last at least two years.

Clearly, Harvard was leading the way in setting higher standards. In a 1901 report to the American Association of Law Schools, Abbott found that most students considered that attending a professional school for two years after four years of undergraduate studies was too long (Abbott, 1901:509; Packer & Ehrlich, 1972). In 1921, the American Bar Association recommended that admission of a candidate to the bar should require completion of general university or college studies and three years of full-time professional study in a certified law school. As a result of these admission requirements, which states progressively adopted, legal studies in the United States became at least relatively standardized. Thus, despite the lack of a central governmental body, by 1925 the requirements and the style that Harvard had promoted became the model to be followed throughout the United States. One of the means of diffusion was the appointment of Harvard graduates as professors or deans in different schools, where they promoted the Harvard model with missionary zeal (Friedman, 2002:33–39).

Why did the United States opt for such a demanding and expensive university legal education when nothing in its tradition suggested it might take such a path? First is the requirement for a total of seven years of preparation: four years of general university education and three in law school proper. Second, legal education relies primarily on full-time professors. Third, it requires a well-stocked, specialized library. As previously noted, public authorities had no involvement in these matters; the external allies of the law schools were the professional organizations. This shifts the question to the motives of these organizations to support an option that went far beyond the original idea of transplanting the university legal education typical of the civil law tradition, particularly Germany, to the United States, a common law country.

Richard Abel (1989) suggests a self-serving motivation. By supporting a demanding model of legal education as a requirement for entry into the profession, lawyers restricted competition at a time when the rapid growth of the profession could threaten established professionals. The second half of the nineteenth century was a time of mass arrival of immigrants. Established lawyers were mostly white and Protestant, and a demanding legal education helped maintain their control of the profession by excluding recent immigrants, Jews, and those of African, Asian, or Hispanic descent. Of course, the idea can be formulated in another way: meritocratic education can help preserve the prestige and ethical standards of a demanding and selective profession (Roithmayr, 1998).

Observers have also pointed out that the modern university law school developed in conjunction with the large law firms that supported and benefited from the great economic expansion of the United States in the last third of the nineteenth and much of the twentieth century (Gordon, 1983). These firms were interested in bringing in well-educated young people with a certain degree of intellectual maturity. Law school education was valuable not so much because of the content acquired there but because students had been trained to work under pressure, to spin arguments using the language of law, and to be skeptical about rules but not to question values. In other words, they acquired skills, attitudes, and values suitable for work in large law firms. In turn, the partners of these large firms became quite wealthy and made substantial donations to the schools, making it possible to provide this expensive training. A virtuous or vicious cycle was thus created, depending on the perspective from which one views this symbiotic relationship between the most prestigious law schools and the large business law firms.

Thus, the interpretation of these changes is subject to a variety of analyses, but what is beyond doubt is the direction of the change. The system was transformed from one of very low academic demands to one of high performance requirements. The law professor emerged as a new occupational category and gained a high place in a new professional stratification, at the top of which were partners in large business law firms (Garth & Schaffer, 2022). The law curriculum has remained much the same, with a first year devoted to the basics of law and inculcating the values, attitudes, and ways of reasoning that are considered proper for lawyers (Mertz, 2007). Courses in the second and third years are mostly electives, and the offerings vary greatly over time and place.

Although Langdell's design constitutes the oldest and most persistent layer of the modern US law school in both the curriculum and the structure of the school itself (Gordon, 2007), this does not mean that all his ideas have been accepted. For example, the use of cases in legal education has remained, but not necessarily with the purposes and methodology proposed by Langdell. Abbott (1901:511) justified retaining case study in terms of the unsystematic character of the common law, which makes more systematic and organized study difficult and not particularly useful. Case study also allows for interdisciplinary analysis and for the law student to acquire at least basic knowledge of other disciplines. Macaulay's (2003) casebook and materials are quite different from Langdell's and clearly correspond to another way of viewing the law.

Other ideas were met with resistance and questioning from the time Langdell was active and, of course, after his death. His conception of the law and even the purposes of education and the Socratic class have been the subject of much discussion and have undergone major changes (LaPiana, 1994). Langdell continues to be a controversial figure today, and many scholars have written about his ideas and influences (Gordon, 1995; Kimball, 2004). A contemporary of Langdell, Oliver Wendell Holmes (1841–1935), who was a professor at Harvard for a brief time, a justice of the Supreme Court, and a major figure of legal thought in the United States, emphasized that "the life of law is not logic, but experience" (Holmes, 1897). Realists, sociologists of law, and practitioners of the economic analysis of law all emphasize the seminal character of Holmes's article, which begins with an attack on Langdell's formalism (Fisher, 2006; Posner, 1992). Louis Brandeis, who entered Harvard Law School in 1875 and was later recognized as an author, lawyer, and a justice of the US Supreme Court, declined to teach at Harvard because of his disagreement with Langdell's proposals (LaPiana, 1994).

Even while Langdell was dean, Harvard's approach to legal education included activities and perspectives that do not fit neatly within Langdell's view of legal education. For example, the *Harvard Law Journal* published articles analyzing the legislation and public policy considerations of the day (Grey, 1983). Roscoe Pound (1870–1964) is an instructive figure in this respect. He was a law student at Harvard in 1889. More than half a century later he remembered his professor John Chipman Gray, who began his casebook on property with references to Roman law (Gray, 1908). This piqued Pound's curiosity, and he searched the library for a work on Roman law. Gray disapproved of the text he found and recommended that he read Sohm's work (*Institutions of Roman Law*) in German (Pound, 1951:523). Pound's recollections make clear that there was much more intellectual curiosity than was permitted by the

Langdellian orthodoxy and that there was interest in foreign literature and the history of law.

Pound had already formulated his critique of formalism and put forward his sociolegal theses before he was appointed professor at Harvard in 1910. Later, in 1916, his appointment as dean indicates that Langdellian formalism did not entirely dominate the law school in that period (Kimball & Coquillette, 2020). In 1912 he published an article pointing out the importance of studying the social effects of institutions and legal rules and the importance of reasonable solutions in the law (Pound, 1912). He was also one of the promoters of comparative law in the United States. Pound was dean for more than twenty years (1916–1937), during which time he promoted research and succeeded in creating the doctoral program, but his deanship was affected by successive crises and difficulties, and he had to resign under pressure from professors.

The so-called American realists (because of their opposition to Langdellian formalism) constituted a strong current of legal thought in the United States. Holmes and Pound are generally considered part of this trend, which included Llewellyn, Frank, Oliphant, Moore, Cohen, and several others. In reality, Holmes and Pound, and other authors critical of formalism, such as Joseph Bingham, predate the flowering of the realist movement. Pound called his proposal sociological jurisprudence and argued against some realists (Hull, 1995).

The realists were especially strong at Columbia and also at Yale, much more so than at Harvard (Gordon, 2004; Kalman, 1986).[9] They were severely critical of Langdell and his method. Jerome Frank (1931) made harsh criticisms and proposed, along with other realists, to replace the case method with clinical education. Llewellyn characterized law school in the United States in these words: "it blinds, it stumbles, it conveyorbelts, it mutilates, and it empties" (Llewellyn, 1935:658). He criticized Langdell for failing to consider what legal professionals actually do and how best to prepare them to perform their various tasks. He compared legal education in the United States with that in Germany and noted that basic education there was very theoretical but that graduates had to undergo three years of internship to become familiar with the various legal professions and had to pass a second professional examination. He also compared legal education with medical education to help justify the need for practical training (Llewellyn, 1930). The realists' proposals met with a poor reception when they were formulated (Kalman, 1986, 2005:19). The general mood was to consider them too controversial, loose, and impractical.

The realists' call for the use of social sciences and the force of their critique of formalism declined in salience during the 1940s and 1950s, but their criticism weakened formalist thought because it became clearer that this method isolated law from social life in ways that were detrimental. Law began to be seen in relation to the economic and social interests at stake, to the public policies to which it responds, and to the fundamental principles of the law. One analysis of legal thought in the United States (Kennedy & Fisher, 2006) calls this trend "legal process, policy and principles"; others prefer to call the trend "postrealist." In a controversial and highly resonant article Lasswell & McDougal (1943) emphasized the importance of linking legal education with public policy (McDougal, 1947).

The best-known postrealist was Lon L. Fuller (1902–1978), a disciple of Joseph Bingham at Stanford and later a professor at Harvard for forty years. He sided with Pound in his dispute with Llewellyn and is generally recognized as one of the leading philosophers of law in the United States (Summers, 1984). He made very important contributions to contract law and the philosophy of law. Professors of the postrealist persuasion also used case analysis, but not to find the principles embedded in decisions and then to draw deductions from them. Rather, they argued that cases are useful for analyzing the public policies at stake and the political, economic, or social consequences of decisions. In this sense, they were opposed to Langdell's formalism, without showing enthusiasm for the use of social sciences advocated by the realists (Feldman, 2004).

Fuller wrote extensively on legal education. In his 1948 article, he found the state of legal education in the United States unsatisfactory. He argued that one cannot appreciate the actual legal process by focusing on judicial decisions. He distinguished two fundamental processes: adjudication, which we would call dispute resolution, and legislation, which he defined broadly as rule making and includes contracts and wills, as well as legislation proper. Other disciplines can be auxiliary in this second task. An interdisciplinary approach thus has a place in legal education, but it must have an auxiliary character so as not to lose focus on what belongs in the domain of lawyers. This perspective also insists on the ethical dimension of decision-making processes in law. The discussion of cases and problems is central to these purposes of legal education (Fuller, 1948).

In his 1950 article, Fuller noted that in his time there was a consensus that the purpose of legal education could not be the transmission of information. There are two fundamental themes in his writings in the area: the purpose of education is to stimulate creative thinking and to educate for freedom. The second theme is the recovery of the ethical dimension of law, something that Langdell and the formalists dismissed (Fuller, 1950).

Robert Gordon (1989:65) gives a firsthand account of what Fuller's classes were like: "My contracts teacher, Lon Fuller, was a master of this kind of situational variation: the challenge in his class was to locate in each case the crucial fact that gave the clue to how policies and equities should be balanced in that case." In this way, the correct position was found.

As Gordon (1989) points out, the casebooks abounded in judgments that reached opposite decisions despite quite similar factual situations. The purpose of case studies was not to teach respect for judges and judicial decisions, which, according to Gordon, characterized English legal education. Postrealists, realists, and formalists did not emphasize the judgments that shaped the law or strive to teach the legal rules. Rather, they sought ways of approaching law that might lead to criticism of judges' decisions but that, in the end, could show a certain rationality of law and justify almost any decision on the basis of some public policy.

According to Gordon (1989), most postrealists insisted on the autonomy of law. From this perspective, professors, lawyers, and law students should avoid the temptation to be economists or sociologists or to go deeper into those disciplines. Or at any rate, it was not necessary for them to do so. However, the exceptions to this generalization among the postrealists are important, and many of them integrated social sciences analysis in the study of law. One of them is James Willard Hurst (1910–1997). He had an enormous influence among his students and young colleagues at the University of Wisconsin. He is considered to have changed the field of legal history by relating it to social and economic history and to have been a major influence on the sociology of law.[10] Fuller himself was interested in the sociology and anthropology of law.[11]

Since the 1960s, the fervor for the use of other social sciences for the analysis of law has been evident. Today's law schools, especially in the most prestigious universities, are varied in the methods they propose for legal analysis, in part because of the prominence given to the use of methods from other social sciences. There are those who privilege economic analysis (law and economics), sociology and anthropology (law and society), and language and rhetoric (law and literature), or those who choose specific fields to which they are oriented.

From the 1970s onward, the so-called critical legal studies movement became popular and generated much controversy and conflict within law schools (Kalman, 1987; Kennedy, 2004; Pérez Lledó, 1996; Unger, 1986). This movement was interested in highlighting the ideological elements in both the rules of law and intellectual works on law. Even more recently, scholars have shown an interest in the implications for law of advances in science and technology (law and technology), in the distortions implied in the formulation and application of law by racial attitudes and prejudices (critical race theory), or in the treatment of women and people with different sexual and gender identities (feminist jurisprudence). The history of law and the study of foreign rights or comparative legal cultures are also flourishing. These varied approaches generate novel ways of examining the law, competition for research resources, and sometimes also conflict within law schools, which are very different places from the one imagined by Langdell.

The different orientations regarding the analysis of the law naturally have implications for legal education. For example, for his course on the philosophy of law, Fuller wrote "cases" that are hypothetical problems to illustrate the main positions on law and to encourage students to reflect. One of them (*The case of speluncean explorers*) has acquired wide circulation in Spanish in the translation of Genaro Carrió (Fuller, 1961). Casebooks have changed substantially, and the most frequent title today refers to cases and materials, because, in addition to judicial decisions, they may refer to legislative choices and to readings that allow for a better understanding of the economic, social, or political substrate of the problem. Many of these materials come from other social sciences or from political disputes. The legal literature published in law school journals incorporates the approach of other social sciences; that is, it has become more interdisciplinary. Moreover, there are a good number of journals that directly define themselves as interdisciplinary, such as the *Law and Society Review*, the *Journal of Law and Economics, Law and Social Inquiry*, and the *Journal of Empirical Legal Studies.*

The social climate of law schools has been another area of significant change. Most law schools have shifted significantly from the atmosphere of competition and faculty authoritarianism that was often characteristic of the Socratic class. The publication of Duncan Kennedy's (1971) early article, published a year after his graduation from Yale Law School, and the novels-turned-movies about the first year of law school and the stress that students suffered, have generated lively discussion and made professors more aware of the negative effects they can have on students.[12] The depiction of US law schools, at least those at the high end of the rankings, are very different from what they were in the 1950s or 1960s.[13]

These changes have also implied a change in the position of US legal education in the global academic environment. Until the 1950s, the law school of the University of Paris could boast of being the legal capital of the world (Halpérin, 2011). Law schools in the United States, especially Harvard, had attracted the attention of some European professors, but they generally considered them adaptations of European legal education, especially German or French, and still had a long way to go to reach the excellence of their models (Bartie & Sandomierski, 2021; Rheinstein, 1938; Valeur, 1928). From that decade onward, the renewal of legal education in the major US law schools and their economic strength made them more attractive to students and scholars from Europe and the rest of the world. The international character of law and the comparative approach to law are emphasized. Professors and young graduates appreciate and boast of the international experience. This internationalization is discussed in the next chapter.

III

Transnationalization and Globalization

The second half of the twentieth century has been called a period of transnationalization. Multinational companies expanded around the world. With them, forms of production and consumption, as well as a multitude of cultural products such as movies, TV series, soap operas, and tourism increased economic and personal relationships between different countries and spread information and shared ideas much more quickly than in the past (Sunkel & Fuenzalida, 1979). Starting in the 1990s, the phenomenon gained new momentum with the spread of the internet; trade and relationships of all kinds between people from different countries increased and intensified rapidly. The fall of the barriers imposed by the Soviet bloc and by China's isolationism made exchanges more universal. Hence, the term "globalization" was used because transnationalization spread to all continents. At the same time, technological changes resulted in the perception of accelerated and widespread transformations (Giddens, 2000). Some distinguish between transnationalization (or internationalization) and globalization as distinctive phenomena with different value (Jamin & vanCaenegen, 2016:4). This work does not make this distinction; rather, these phenomena are considered stages of the same process.

Transnationalization and globalization have had significant impacts on law and politics. International organizations have grown rapidly and have become largely autonomous sources of law. These include organizations directly linked to law, such as the International Institute for the Unification of the Private Law (UNIDROIT), the United Nations Commission on International Trade Law (UNCITRAL) , the International Court of Justice, the European Court of Human Rights, the Inter-American Court of Human Rights, the International Court of Arbitration of the International Chamber of Commerce, the European Court of Justice, and the International Criminal Court. They also include organizations specializing in certain matters that seem distinct from the law but are very important to it, such as the International Labour Organization, the World Trade Organization, UNESCO, the International Monetary Fund, and the World Bank. These organizations prepare international treaties, develop models of legislation and contracts, resolve conflicts, create jurisprudence, and evaluate respect for human rights, the rule of law, national legislation, and international treaties. It can no longer be said that the law is mainly produced and relevant only within nations. Certainly, national states are a source of legislation and other legal norms, and national courts continue to have important weight in the application of formal law. Most lawyers work only with national law and use only local language (Friedman, 2001). The same applies to many law schools, but a growing number of law schools are attentive to international or global developments (Garth & Schaffer, 2022), and an important subset of lawyers requires more varied knowledge than national law.

The internationalization of law firms constitutes a very important development. International firms, that is, those with offices in different countries, have grown enormously in number and size. Around 1950, almost all law firms were national and small. By 2021, international firms were counted in the thousands, and the largest ones had ten thousand or more lawyers (Gómez & Galanter, 2020; Gómez & Pérez-Perdomo, 2018). Furthermore, firms that are seemingly national may participate in international networks that meet periodically, communicate among themselves, and refer clients reciprocally.[1] The practice of law has become international to the point that mastery of multiple languages, especially English, and some familiarity with other legal cultures are necessary or important credentials for working in many firms, including national ones. Many of the most important cases have components from different countries, including different legal traditions (Gómez, 2021).

The field of human rights has become fundamental in global legal systems. Although its origins date to the eighteenth century or earlier, the modern development of human rights intensified after World War II. Since then, international treaties have multiplied, many international organizations have been created, and an enormous literature has flourished. Among the international organizations are the Human Rights Council, created by the United Nations, and the High Commissioner for Human Rights, linked to the UN Secretary-General. These are independent organizations and both are very important worldwide. The European Court of Human Rights, the Inter-American Commission on Human Rights, and the Inter-American Court of Human Rights are among the many international organizations in the field. Nongovernmental organizations such as Amnesty International and Human Rights Watch issue reports that are publicized worldwide, make headlines in many news outlets, and draw the attention of national governments. Furthermore, it can be said that there is a culture of human rights, meaning that the idea that we have rights that are above the state and that we can claim against it, has penetrated the population and even governments that are not willing to respect those rights (Friedman, 2011). For a transnational corporation, it is crucial to ensure that human rights are respected, even in jurisdictions where there may be no legal or political consequences for failing to do so. A company can risk significant damage to its reputation if it is discovered that its suppliers in far-off countries are using child or slave labor or causing severe environmental damage.

The rule of law has also become a universal model that is expected to be adopted by countries. Countries are expected to have a constitution that establishes the separation or relative independence of public powers, and leaders are expected to respect the limits of their authority, including the conduct of democratic, free, and fair elections. Respect for human rights is part of this model. However, this model is often more honored in the breach than in practice. Even in traditionally democratic countries, leaders have disregarded or attempted to disregard election results. There have also been reports in the United States of children being separated from their parents and locked in cages. In many countries, certain social groups are subject to discrimination. The groups may vary from one society to another, but cruel treatment, which involves members of these social groups suffering serious human rights violations, is common. There are more than a few rulers who have become increasingly authoritarian and disrespectful of the rights of citizens, even though they speak the language of human rights (Friedman, 2011).

Perhaps it is most worrying that human rights violators often enjoy broad political and social sympathies. Authoritarian rulers and dictators are frequently popular among significant segments of the population, even after they have been removed from power. Punishing human rights violators, including torturers, is not always easy, as the judicial or transitional justice systems have limited capacity to process and punish offenders, especially when they are numerous or widely popular.

Also countering globalization is a growing sense of nationalism, such as the Brexit movement that led the United Kingdom to leave the European Union or the movement for Catalan independence, which would result in its separation from Spain and the European Union. The increasing waves of immigrants, one manifestation of globalization, have led many countries to strengthen their national borders. More recently, the COVID-19 pandemic led national states to reactivate their border controls, even between countries that had previously abolished reciprocal borders in a common economic space. These are some of the serious limitations to the functioning of the rule of law and to the understanding that we live in an increasingly interconnected world. Against this backdrop, what is new is that groups with growing importance are devoting attention and effort to human rights, international business, and the transnational aspects of law. Law can be seen as the product of a constant struggle (Jhering, 1872/1976), and for that reason, perhaps one can never speak of a definitive result.

Another aspect worth highlighting is the significant internationalization of law school faculties. This varies from country to country, but it is common for professors to pursue postgraduate studies in other countries, to visit foreign universities for teaching or research projects, and to publish in law journals in different countries and languages. In most cases, internationalization is appreciated in the development of a professor's career (Jamin & van Caenegen, 2016). The United States is one of the countries that has attracted a significant flow of such visitors. Its law schools attract a growing number of graduates from different countries, and many of the dominant legal ideas in the United States have rapid diffusion in the world. This situation can lead to the view that globalization, especially in law and legal education, is a process of Americanization (Garth & Schaffer, 2022; Dezalay & Garth, 2021). On the contrary, this chapter argues that influence is not a one-way movement and that globalization or internationalization has involved, initially, a reform process in US law schools that continues to operate, as well as subsequent adaptations of those reforms in many other countries.

The key issues in this chapter are whether law schools have incorporated the international dimension of law into their curricula, whether they are preparing students for the new type of practice in which legal professionals encounter different legal cultures, and whether they are doing anything to strengthen the value their students place on the rule of law and human rights. The question is, ultimately, whether students understand that the law is not just a set of coercible norms but must be understood in its context and purposes and whether law school graduates are able to practice law in other countries or in the international sphere. Where the law school education is narrowly national and formalist, another possibility is that graduates have found ways to remedy their limited training.

PALACE WARS IN THE LAW SCHOOLS

Law schools have been training centers for political elites in many countries in Latin America and Europe, making the law curriculum politically relevant and frequently subject to political conflicts. As we have seen, this is also true for the United States. In our time, transformations in society and the law create added tension for law schools due to conflicting perceptions of the need for change, of the changes in the legal education, and of the law itself. The themes of curriculum reform generally include pedagogical proposals that have a political background and that translate into struggles for power within educational institutions. The previous chapters have alluded to this at some moments in history that we have analyzed, although political conflicts and struggles have not been a primary focus. For the contemporary period and with reference to Latin America, Dezalay & Garth (2002) have called these conflicts "palace wars." This term comes from the past, when hidden conflicts with poison and daggers, or more frequently, deceit or gossip, occurred in the palaces of kings and popes. Law schools lack the splendor of palaces, but they are closed social spaces in which members of an elite move. In this case, the elite consists of the law professors and administrators, with some student involvement.

In the United States, with the emergence of legal realists, critical legal studies, critical race theory, and feminist jurisprudence in law schools such as Harvard, Columbia, Yale, and Stanford, the conflict has manifested itself in harsh criticism of judicial decisions and colleagues' work. What interests us particularly here is the impact of those conflicts on the educational curriculum, whether it be the offering of particular subjects and activities, research orientation issues, or the methods and educational resources to be used. The tenure or permanence of professors was especially controversial in these universities. The conflicts often have a political element, but they are generally not struggles to transform the state. It is therefore doubtful that change in the state structure has been the concern of those who propose reforms of legal education in the United States or any other country. However, it must be recognized that discussions of legal education can have a political impact in the medium term and that different approaches to legal studies can be intertwined with ideological struggles or personal ambitions.

The important thing to highlight is that professors in the United States, at least in several law schools, were successful in fighting the formalist approach at an earlier point than were Europeans and Latin Americans. As a result, in addition to the judicial decisions that were typical of the Langdellian tradition, a variety of materials were incorporated into the didactic literature. Early on, the law curricula included subjects aimed at competencies such as negotiation, contract drafting, and litigation. Clinical education became a common element. In addition, economic or social analysis of law and the consideration of law as part of public policies were novel and helped make legal studies more attractive, even for foreign students.

These innovations led to a new appreciation of American legal education. Even by the mid-twentieth century, European comparativists had not understood the orientation of American legal education or the transformations that occurred in response to the realist movement. The works of Charles Eisenmann (1954), which outlined the panorama of legal education in the world, and André Tunc (1964), in his study of the legal system of the United States, showed a lack of understanding of or even interest in US legal education. In contrast, the situation was different in Latin America. For example, the lecture of San Tiago Dantas (1955) demonstrates that he was well informed about what law schools in the United States were doing, and his proposal for reform corresponded with the new trends in US legal education.[2] Furthermore, he argued that the US law schools were producing better lawyers and that those lawyers were more successful in the world. During this period, American lawyers were working in Latin America, and US law firms were beginning to expand (Gómez, 2021; Gómez & Pérez-Perdomo, 2018; Pérez-Perdomo, 2020b).

The San Tiago Dantas lecture (1955), later turned into an article, struck a particularly sensitive chord. The criticisms of legal education he articulated were not new. They basically coincided with those of Colmo (1915), but there were several elements that made them especially pointed. For example, Dantas noticed that Brazilian lawyers were not important in large international negotiations. The handling of national codes, which was the expertise of Brazilian lawyers, was irrelevant to international business. Instead, US lawyers were handling such negotiations, even though US corporations were not parties to them. In addition, Dantas offered clear proposals: legal education needed to go beyond codes, to use cases, to be interdisciplinary, and to engage students more actively. Dantas collected ideas that were in the air, and ultimately, the discussion on legal education in the following decades focused on these ideas and issues. In Brazil, the resonance was immediate (Bastos, 2000:250ss; Rosenn, 1969:273; Steiner, 1971).

Clearly, these ideas were shared by a significant number of Latin American leaders of legal education at the time. Between 1959 and 1964, four Latin American conferences were organized, and their minutes testify to the concerns of the attending deans of faculties and directors of law schools. The proposed reforms included the introduction of class discussion and the use of cases, seminar techniques, and an interdisciplinary approach (Brown, 1961; Wilson, 1989:393). In 1974, a fifth conference was held. Among the conclusions of this conference (Riesco, 1976) was the rejection of the professors' lectures as the main teaching method, the promotion of research seminars, and the adoption of the case method, and the study of problems and records. In the early 1970s, García La Guardia (1976) recognized a consensus on the reforms that were considered necessary. In Mexico, the influential jurist Fix-Zamudio (1976) also highlighted the concern that Latin American law schools only encouraged the ability to memorize texts.

It is worth noting that the conception of law as a coherent normative system based on the rules approved by the state, although dominant in Latin American legal education during the first half of the century, faced criticisms similar to those that had been articulated in Europe since the beginning of the twentieth century. In response to growing criticisms, interest in the reform of the university structures and teaching of law intensified, but the weight of tradition made change difficult.

The reformers received unexpected support in the 1960s in the form of the so-called law and development programs promoted by the Ford Foundation, the US Agency for International Development (USAID), and the International Legal Center (Gardner, 1980). The programs supported reform of legal studies in Costa Rica (1965), Brazil (1966), Chile (1967), Peru (1967), and Colombia (1969). The programs consisted of US law professors' visits to these countries to work with local professors, visits by Latin American professors to US law schools, meetings of professors to discuss legal education reform issues, and donations of equipment such as photocopy machines that allowed for the printing of teaching materials. The reformers received support, but the resistance of conservative educators and political revolutionaries intensified because of the US involvement. Some saw the programs as instruments of US imperialism that aimed to destroy the foundations of the Latin American civil law tradition. Teaching through lectures and explanation of the codes was considered essential to this tradition. Within a few years, the missionary-professors acknowledged their failure to change the culture of Latin American law schools and blamed themselves for their naïveté, ethnocentrism, and lack of a solid theoretical basis for change (Trubek and Galanter, 1974:1065). John Merryman directed other projects focused more on collaborative research work between Latin American,

European, and US professors (Merryman, 2000a, 2000b; Merryman, Clark & Friedman, 1979).

Lynch (1981) offers a very convincing explanation of the failure of these efforts in Colombia, and the explanation may extend to all Latin America. The 1970s was a decade of urbanization, economic growth, and great expansion of the interventionist state. There was a strong demographic pressure on law schools to expand, and there were ample jobs for law graduates as lawyers or government officials. Only a few of the most prominent lawyers were concerned that lawyers were ill equipped to work in planning and other important tasks of the interventionist state. Many felt that they were starting their professional life without adequate preparation, but that did not hinder them from obtaining employment. From this perspective, law schools had to worry more about how to handle the avalanche of students than about changing educational methodology or teaching approaches. In other words, in the midst of success, there was no reason to change.

In contrast, Dezalay and Garth (2002) offer an argument related to power struggles between different groups. They argue that the law and development movement was an effort to increase the relevance of lawyers and of their knowledge vis-à-vis economists and, more generally, to transplant to Latin America institutional arrangements developed in the United States: a struggle for power. However, this argument does not consider that efforts to reform legal education began half a century earlier. The struggle for power is surely always present in social relations, but interpreting the efforts of professors to better understand the operation of law and to better educate students as primarily a struggle for power falsifies a much richer history. In the case of Héctor Fix-Zamudio in Mexico, for example, we may ask whether his dedication to a way of understanding the law and his opinions on legal education were motivated by ambitions of power. If we examine his biography, that does not seem to be the case (Pérez-Perdomo, 2012). Perhaps Fix-Zamudio is an exceptional case, but to test this, we would need to evaluate the collective biography of those who have driven reforms in legal education and research in Latin America. Young professors were undoubtedly more likely to have an interest in reforms, and older ones with less international exposure were more resistant. This does not necessarily reflect a greater power ambition among the younger professors but, in many cases, a genuine search for better educational methods and richer approaches and methods in research among those whose own educational experiences were fresher.

Proposals for overall reform of legal education were rejected by most law schools because of the opposition of tradition-minded professors. However, some professors maintained an interest in reform and made changes to their teaching methodology or course content, taking advantage of academic freedom. Several innovative professors were expelled from universities, but many stayed and continued to try new approaches at an individual level. As demand for legal studies remained high in the 1980s and beyond, new law schools were established, especially in private universities. In this situation, innovators were able to reintegrate into academic life relatively quickly. Professors who were expelled for promoting innovations and innovators who felt uncomfortable in traditional schools were active in the formation of new law schools or in teaching in them.[3] Several of these schools have had a commitment to innovation, likely in order to differentiate themselves from established schools and to compete for the top students.

In the 1980s and beyond, a significant number of young graduates chose to pursue master's or doctoral studies in universities in the United States and Europe. They became familiar with other approaches to the law and legal education. This has had a significant impact largely because those interested in new approaches found schools interested in receiving them. The effect of the various innovations underway is that we can no longer speak of a uniform Latin American legal education; variety is the rule (Gonzales Mantilla, 2018). This is also true if we reduce the geographic framework to Brazil (Rodrigues & Junqueira, 2002), Mexico (Pérez Hurtado, 2009), Peru (Gonzales Mantilla, 2008; Zolezzi, 2017), or Venezuela (Pérez-Perdomo, 2018). Law schools, their styles, and purposes represent a wide range of approaches. The result has been a stratification of law schools and of lawyers, as well as a certain rupture of the professional legal culture of these countries, a topic that is beyond the scope of the present analysis.

An argument that must be confronted more directly is related to the role of imperialism. Some have viewed changes in legal education as part of the policies of colonial or neocolonial powers (Dezalay & Garth,

2002, 2019; Gardner, 1980; Garth & Schaffer, 2022). It is well known that the United States tried to spread its model of legal education in the 1960s, and that previously England and France attempted to spread their way of seeing the law in the countries they colonized. In the case of the United States, the declared motivation was that changing the education of the political elite would promote the modernization of the country—or, the skeptic might say, the goal was to make the elite more friendly to the United States and its interests. We have already seen that the US effort was short-lived (Trubek & Galanter, 1974), and it is noteworthy that interest in studying in the United States increased in the decades that followed the collapse of those efforts, even though the US government and foundations were not particularly interested in funding Latin American law graduates for studying in the US. Furthermore, the historical experiences analyzed here do not show that changes in legal education always reflected imperial policies. In Latin America in the early nineteenth century, the reform of legal education was aimed at cultural independence from Spain and Portugal, the colonial powers. Latin American reformers were interested in access to modern ideas. In the United States, the reforms undertaken by Harvard around 1870 were influenced by Germany, but not because Germany had any imperial aims in the United States.

Dissatisfaction with legal formalism and its consequences for legal education was present in Latin America and Europe from the beginning of the twentieth century and even before that among intellectual jurists. Dantas offers an example. His interest in a more social conception of law appeared early in his life, and his efforts to change legal education caused conflicts with students and colleagues. His 1955 lecture showed that he was aware of the changes in legal education and the legal profession in the United States and believed that adopting some of those changes would help Brazil's development. He was a leftist, and during his tenure as minister of foreign affairs, he opposed US policy in Cuba and helped Brazil establish diplomatic relations with the Soviet Union. Dantas is an example, and one cannot generalize from him, but it is probably healthy to consider the thinking and interests of Latin Americans and Europeans themselves in efforts to reform legal education, and not to see these reforms only as imposed by an imperial power.

To analyze the impact of US legal education in the world, it is also important to consider the decisions of those interested in what these law schools offer, that is, students who might be considering attendance. Some Latin American and European graduates with an interest in an academic career may do so out of a genuine intellectual interest in experiencing a different way of approaching the law and a desire to experience the significant resources that a number of US universities have to offer. Other graduates may perceive that studying in these schools can give them an edge on entering a law firm or, more generally, developing a more international professional practice. The first group is likely less numerous but more important in terms of their impact on legal education. As law professors, they can spread ideas and styles to a considerably larger group.

In Latin America, resistance to legal education reform weakened in the 1980s and 1990s with the creation of new, mostly private universities. This was part of a general policy of liberalizing university education and was especially important for legal education. Several law schools aspired to compete in quality with the more recognized traditional ones. To do this, they opted for more modern academic structures and curricula. Nontraditional professors who had been expelled from traditional universities or marginalized in them found a new niche.

Educational projects differ depending on the law school. Pérez-Perdomo and Gómez (2008) compiled descriptive essays on experiences of legal education renewal in Argentina, Brazil, Chile, Colombia, Mexico, and Venezuela (Gómez 2018). More recently, Ghirardi (2021) analyzed the Brazilian law schools and found new approaches that included the introduction of legal clinics, guided internships, research projects, and curricular flexibility. Everywhere, in courses that retained traditional titles, cases or problems and participatory classes were introduced. The influence of US legal education is apparent but with important adaptations or reservations. Legal education has been maintained at the undergraduate level with a duration of four to five years. Courses such as Roman law, legal history, legal sociology, and legal philosophy have remained mandatory in many curricula, although their contents may have changed substantially.

Europe maintained its traditional approach to legal education for longer than Latin America, in part because state-supported universities carry much more weight and function as a large system that ensures greater uniformity. Pérez Lledó (2003) described legal education in Spain at the end of the twentieth century as substantially traditional in approach, that is, lecture-based, characterized by separation of disciplines, and reflecting little attention from professors to teaching tasks. However, new law schools have been developed in Spain, France, Germany, and the Netherlands that break with these traditions (Atienza, 2016). Some of these are highlighted later in the chapter.

As we have seen, the growth of large international law firms has placed a premium on lawyers who are multilingual and familiar with the legal cultures of different countries. Law professors and law students are now more exposed to different legal cultures. In particular, US law schools have experienced an influx of foreign students, with consequences in both directions for institutions and students. The next section addresses how the interest in receiving foreign students and their increased presence have influenced US legal education and how the internationalization of law and legal education is having an important impact everywhere, particularly in Latin America (Dezalay & Garth 2019, 2021, Garth & Schaffer 2022).

LOST IN TRANSLATION? LATIN AMERICAN AND EUROPEAN LAWYERS IN US LAW SCHOOLS

The presence of law graduates trained in the civil law tradition as students in US law schools raises the issue of the degree of adaptability from one legal tradition to another. If these traditions have distinctive views of the law and if the educational methods differ substantially between them, Latin American and European graduates could face difficult challenges, and their experience in the United States could end up having little benefit. These foreign graduate students might feel completely lost in US law schools, just as the American actor in the movie *Lost in Translation* (Coppola, 2003) experiences severe culture shock while filming a commercial in Tokyo.

As we have seen in the previous section, this scenario is not purely theoretical. Beginning in the mid-1960s, law graduates from Latin America and Europe have been pursuing further legal studies in the best-known universities in the United States, and these universities have been interested in receiving them. Damaska (1968) reacted to the situation by observing that good European legal education provided a systematic understanding of the legal system and the conceptual language of law.[4] In his view, this was the grammar of law. In contrast, in US law schools, legal reasoning was learned, but little attention was paid to the architecture of the system, and relatively little attention was paid to conceptual elaboration. In short, Damaska expected lawyers educated in the civil law tradition to face serious difficulties in American law schools; beyond the linguistic barrier, they would also need help understanding a different legal culture.

John H. Merryman (1974) conducted a similar analysis that incorporated social elements.[5] He compared law schools institutionally and showed that in the civil law tradition, law studies were undergraduate and tended toward mass education. In the United States, the best schools received graduate students from other disciplines and competed for the top students. Professors paid more attention to education and used case studies and class discussions as the predominant method, while in the civil law tradition, lectures by the professor and law manuals, which were in fact written versions of the lectures, predominated. Merryman also highlighted the attention paid in US law schools to the economic and social context in which law was produced or interpreted. His analysis valued US law schools as superior. Although Merryman did not directly address the difficulties that graduates of the civil law tradition would face in the United States, the conclusion would be similar to that of Damaska, despite the difference in their starting point and analytic approach. We might expect graduates of the civil law tradition to experience enormous difficulties in the transfer to the US legal education system.

Those difficulties or "trials and tribulations of adjustment," as Damaska calls them, do exist and are surely significant. Lazarus-Black, working with small samples, found that foreign students do indeed face challenges in the transition to a different legal tradition and teaching model (Lazarus-Black, 2017; Lazarus-Black & Globokar, 2015). Others have found that students give these challenges less importance (Vides et al., 2011). The tribulations may be more or less severe depending on the case, but clearly, they do not have sufficient severity to have prevented the increasing flow of graduates in law from different countries of the civil law tradition to continue their studies in the United States. They number in the thousands every year. Between 2000 and 2012, the number of foreign law graduates taking master's, doctoral, or professional (JD) programs increased by 52 percent. Similarly, people with a first degree outside the United States who took bar exams increased substantially (Silver, 2013). This chapter is particularly interested in Latin Americans, but the flow also includes countries from continental Europe, Asia, and Africa. It is notable that the reverse flow has not occurred, at least not in comparable numbers. Few law graduates from the United States have considered studies in countries of the civil law tradition, especially in Latin America.

How can we explain this continuing flow, and in particular, why do adjustment challenges not discourage foreign law graduates? Globalization is a simple answer, perhaps true but unsatisfactory for all that it fails to explain. Increased contacts between the countries of the world make other countries and cultures seem less strange or exotic, and graduate-level law students can arrive prepared in the language and aware of the different ways of thinking about law. Globalization can mitigate the culture shock, but it does not explain the attraction of US law schools or the area of convergence.

The circumstances characterizing the development of law schools in the United States and in the civil law tradition are one aspect of this situation that we must not overlook. In the civil law tradition, beginning in the nineteenth century, law schools aimed to teach national law. Hence, the organization of the code was adopted, or systems were constructed that allowed for the solution of cases by applying deductive reasoning, always thinking within a national framework. For this reason, these law schools have limited appeal for those who plan to practice the profession in another country or for law graduates from other countries or traditions interested in broadening their expertise. In the United States, national (federal) law has a relatively limited domain; most cases are decided by state courts applying the law of that state. The applicable regulations can differ significantly from one state to another. Harvard, and later the other major law schools, expected to train lawyers who could practice in any state, that is, who could relate to different legal systems. Hence, the emphasis was first on "reasoning as a lawyer," that is, learning to locate relevant facts and the rules and principles that would lead to a convincing solution. When this was seen as insufficient, an expansion was sought in two directions: through the incorporation of the economic or social context and through the acquisition of other skills such as negotiating, understanding a company's accounts, or presenting arguments. Thus, while European and Latin American professors strove to understand a national legal system as a coherent system and to explain its concepts, the US law schools focused on how to find the relevant rule, how to understand it in its context, and how to solve cases with it (Sullivan, 2007).

Globalization and economic integration have shaken up both legal traditions. The integration of European economies and societies has brought into question the national approach in Europe. Investment, production, and distribution now target a broader European and global market. Law firms and legal education have had to respond to these demands from businesses and society at large. Higher education, in general, has been affected. The Bologna Declaration of 1999 and the Tuning Project have proposed a harmonization of curricula based on, not content taught, but the skills acquired and the equivalence of titles and diplomas (Clark, 1998, 2012:353–360). For legal education, this has meant an enormous upheaval, including in educational methods. The lecture-based class, while good for organizing and transmitting content, must give way to other methods that better develop skills, abilities, and attitudes. The course content itself must be reconsidered, as the national framework is no longer the reference point for law. Many courses have therefore become comparative law courses, such as comparative constitutional law or international business law. So-called soft courses, such as sociology of law, economic analysis of law, legal history, comparative law, and research seminars, have gained new relevance and new content. Many courses are now built around problems; that is, they offer problem-based learning. New programs and renewed institutions have emerged (Heringa, 2011). Here are two examples taken from the websites of European law schools:

> In this programme, you will look at legal problems from a comparative and European perspective, rather than focusing on the solution given in a single legal system. You will study both EU and international law, working in small groups on relevant real-life topics will train you in essential legal skills such

as problem-solving, legal reasoning, pleading and writing . . . (University of Maastricht Law School, curriculum.maastrichtuniversity.nl/education/bachelor/bachelor-european-law-school)

The Sciences Po Law School aims at educating high-caliber law professionals, capable of engaging in a constantly changing professional world . . . Our challenge: to teach students law, through an interactive pedagogical method that develops their critical mind and creativity. (L'École de Droit de Sciences Po, sciencespo.fr/ecole-de-droit/en.html)

It should be noted that Sciences Po requires a university degree and that the studies last three years. Some courses are offered in English, which brings it very close to the equivalent law schools in the United States. The establishment of this school had the support of the leading business law firms in Paris, which, according to the website, continue to support it. It faced enormous resistance from existing law schools for its new approach. The "palace war" was so serious that it became a public and judicial matter (Jamin, 2012), and the conflict had to be resolved by the Conseil d'État, the supreme administrative court in France.

These are not unique or exceptional schools. The Bucerius Law School at the University of Berlin, the Instituto Empresa in Madrid, and other institutions also offer a similar education. However, the direction is not the one that most law schools have taken, and there is significant resistance to change in many of them. In contrast, pressure from law firms and the European Union, generally transmitted by the education ministries of the countries, is also important in reform efforts.

In Latin America, the movement for change began earlier, and the topic continues to be debated, but the need for change has been felt with less urgency than in Europe, where economic integration and globalization have exerted much more intense pressure. Resistance also seems to be less pronounced. However, the overall result is not very different—a very diverse legal education in law schools that represent educational projects with very different orientations. Quality is also very uneven. An example of a modern conception of a law school is offered by the law degree program at Centro de Investigación y Docencia Económicas (CIDE) in Mexico. This institution was initially a research and teaching center in economics and has become a university with programs in economics, political science, history, and law. The website offers the following description: "The program emphasizes the importance of the key skills of the legal profession, together with a solid foundation of inter-disciplinary knowledge. Our activity-based teaching methods stem from the conviction that students should take the lead role in their intellectual and professional formation" (see the website cide.edu/programa.derecho).

Several other law schools in Mexico and other Latin American coun-tries are undertaking projects in a similar direction to that proposed by CIDE. The potential difficulties of adjustment for Latin American graduates in US law schools will depend greatly on their law school of origin and whether they have already been exposed to a way of thinking that differs from the traditional civil law tradition, to the study of cases and problems, and to participation in class sessions. The adjustment pro-cess also depends on the receiving US law school, as these are also not homogeneous.

In summary, from the 1970s onward, young graduates from con-tinental Europe and Latin America began to arrive at law schools in the United States to take master's and, to a much lesser extent, doctoral programs. Thousands of law graduates from countries of the civil law tradition have made that move every year. The difficulty in adapting to a different legal tradition in legal education has been less than expected (Silver, 2013). Naturally, this does not imply that there are no challenges. The important thing is that law graduates from the civil law tradition have found it useful to familiarize themselves with US law, and mas-ter's courses have offered them the opportunity to do so (Pérez-Perdomo, 2019). The adaptation to a new type of legal education has been less pain-ful than Damaska expected.

In general, it can be said that law schools in the United States have adapted to receive graduates from other cultures. It is in their institu-tional and economic interest to do so. In some cases, adaptation has been minimal and consists of a one-year master's degree program, which usu-ally offers foreign students an introduction to US law and allows them to take second- and third-year courses that interest them. These courses are often seminars or, in any case, less idiosyncratic than larger first-year classes. Harvard began offering this kind of option relatively early. In the 1970s, it had two programs attended by more than two hundred foreign students, the master's degree and the International Tax Program, which was not initially intended as an academic track but was later transformed into a specialized master's degree program.[6] Such a one-year master's degree program at a good university in the United States is a complement to a legal education and law degree in a country with a civil law tradition, and it may facilitate employment in an international law firm. In other cases, the effort of transformation is much more profound. One example, analyzed by Clark (1998, 2012), is the New York University School of Law. Generally, internationalization programs are well advertised and designed to attract good foreign students or give an international dimension to the legal studies of American students. Such programs may offer courses abroad, often in collaboration with local universities.[7]

Stanford Law School offers an interesting example of the adaptation to an international student enrollment. Until about 1950, it was a prestigious law school in the western United States but fairly traditional in its approach to legal education (Lempert, 2003; Macaulay, 2003).[8] Between 1955 and 1960, under the deanship of Carl Spaeth and the direction of Lawrence F. Ebb, Stanford developed a program for graduates from India.[9] In the 1970s, it developed a program with Chilean universities (Merryman, 2000a), hired Mauro Cappelletti, offered courses on law in different cultures (Barton et al. 1983), and generated the Stanford Law and Development (SLADE) program, a large research project that brought together scholars from Latin America, Italy, and Spain with professors Merryman and Friedman (Merryman 2000b; Merryman, Clark & Friedman, 1979).[10] For his part, Cappelletti directed a vast worldwide project on access to justice, later published in six volumes (Cappelletti & Garth, 1978–1979). David Clark and Bryan Garth, two young graduates who later developed distinguished academic careers in comparative law and sociology of law, participated in these projects.

Until the 1990s, however, Stanford mainly attracted students from the United States. In that decade, the creation of the research-focused, public-policy-oriented master's degree program (Rademacher, 1999), as well as the creation of several master's degree programs focused on novel subjects, attracted a significant number of law graduates from a wide range of countries. Graduates from these programs have made significant impact in their home countries and in the United States. In particular, the research program attracted young professors who later developed successful academic careers. Stanford also reformulated its doctoral program in law, which is primarily attended by international students. By 2019, 20 percent of Stanford's law school students were foreign law graduates, generally with some professional experience, which enriches class discussions for all involved. Those enrolled in the JD program, traditionally for those interested in practicing law in the United States, are much more exposed to the international dimension of law through various types of contact with international institutions. The Franke Global Law Program, for example, embodies that objective.

In summary, globalization has not been a one-way street. It is not just the Americanization of legal education in different countries; legal education in the United States has also been transformed. Clearly, modern-day law schools in the United States, Europe, and Latin America are very different from how they were in the 1960s, when Damaska (1968) published his article.

EDUCATION, PROFESSION, AND SOCIETY

Does globalization imply the homogenization of legal education and the irrelevance of different legal traditions? This would be a hasty and certainly false conclusion. On the contrary, even within each tradition and each country, law schools differ dramatically. Some are more traditional; others seek to modernize or innovate. Some see the law as associated with freedom and rights; others see it as a neutral technology or in the service of the state. There are many intermediate points between these extremes. The innovation that one school seeks may be very different from that of another. Some law schools choose to invest in good teachers, student selection, modern equipment, suitable buildings, and subsidized research. Others cannot or do not want to prioritize such investments. The globalized world is heterogeneous and unequal, and at least in legal education, heterogeneity has actually increased.

The world of legal professionals has also become more differentiated and unequal. One can speak of professional stratification in which some lawyers are very successful, advising businesses of great importance that generally involve multinational investments and production and distribution facilities in several countries. These business lawyers are generally grouped in large or relatively large firms that provide services with continuity, quality, and efficiency. Other lawyers function individually or in small firms (boutiques) and, because of their knowledge and skills, attend to more individualized needs of very important clients. To a large extent, both these categories of lawyers are familiar with different legal cultures, enjoy professional prestige, and earn very high incomes.

In contrast, most lawyers serve domestic clients and deal only with national law (Friedman, 2001). This group includes lawyers who work for the largest employer: national or local government. Some hold positions in the highest spheres of state and politics, but most work in subordinate positions, resulting in further stratification within the group. Overall, for lawyers who work within national borders, success, income, and social status vary widely. Some are successful, with good incomes and social prestige. Others are less successful, and some barely survive and must resort to questionable forms of practice to make ends meet (Pérez-Perdomo, 2006). Some lawyers have become defenders of human rights, and others work tirelessly in the service of authoritarian governments. There are also those with high incomes but negative professional reputations and short lives, such as lawyers for drug traffickers and organized crime in general (Ravelo, 2006). What is notable is that the legal tactics they employ require careful professional efforts (Meneses Reyes, 2018). The legal profession is a kind of large archipelago with islands of different sizes and landscapes. The concept of professional stratification is a shorthand for that complex panorama.

Is there a relationship between legal education and professional success? In the past, when legal education within a country was relatively uniform, professional success depended more on other factors, such as individual characteristics and social or family networks of support. Lawyers also performed relatively similar tasks. That world no longer exists. We might conjecture that the diversification of legal education has made it more determinative of a student's professional career and success. As such, we might imagine a relationship between one's legal education and the island on which one's career unfolds and success and status are achieved. The association does not have to be based only on the formal curriculum of law schools; it may reflect the aspects of socialization they fulfill. For example, professional networks are formed in schools that can then be important for the careers of their graduates. Of course, the strength of the relationship should not be exaggerated; travel is possible between islands. Other factors can intervene, such as gender, the family, and the social networks in which one is embedded, as well as personal strengths and skills.

The current situation suggests that at the top of the stratification of lawyers are graduates from a small number of law schools and individuals who have complemented their education with postgraduate degrees from universities or study centers with a good reputation abroad. Many of these lawyers have practices related to important investments—many of them from multinational companies—or they work directly in international institutions. Unfortunately, empirical studies that would allow this conjecture to be turned into a hypothesis and given a foundation in data are scarce. Pérez-Perdomo (2001) showed that as of about 2000, lawyers from the Venezuelan national oil company (PDVSA), a select group in the legal profession at the time, came from a few law schools. Within the company, those who belonged to the upper echelon and dealt with international business had earned postgraduate degrees abroad and spoke English and other languages. Gómez (2003) found that most lawyers from large firms in Caracas came from just two universities.

The impression is that a similar pattern occurs in other Latin American countries (Gómez & Pérez-Perdomo, 2018), but this has not been quantified. Venezuela currently represents an unusual situation, given the massive emigration that has taken place, which tests the capacity of lawyers to adapt their professional lives to work outside the country where they were trained. For example, in the case of the Universidad Metropolitana of Caracas, a prestigious and innovative university that has a relatively new law school, a follow-up study revealed that most law graduates between 2006 and 2016 worked outside of Venezuela, and approximately half of them had occupations related to law (Capriles & Pérez-Perdomo, 2019). No similar analysis has been done of graduates from other Venezuelan law schools, and as Garth and Schaffer (2022:16) point out, we lack information about where lawyers work and their positions to know more about globalization and stratification.

As previously noted, most professionals surely have a more traditional professional practice, limited to national law and without the need for communication in languages other than their own, and some have great difficulties finding a job market. A conjecture is that the law school of origin, probably also linked to the student's social stratum and their social networks of belonging, will be important in the graduate's career in this part of the professional archipelago as well.

Law schools communicate a way of thinking about the law (or a conception of the law), attitudes toward the norms and institutions of the legal system, and the values of the law, as well as knowledge of the norms and professional skills. This is what we call the professional culture of law. Globalization has not brought the homogenization of this culture, but it has generated diverse professional cultures. It has broken apart national legal cultures. The variety in professional legal culture is not in itself a bad thing. It can play a positive role if it promotes debate regarding ideas and enriches the intellectual climate.

However, this optimistic view of diversity has a limit. If we want a world in which we conduct ourselves in accordance with the principles of the rule of law, in which respect for human rights and harmony with the environment are taken seriously, in short, a more just and democratic world, then legal education must communicate those values and seek to make them shared values in society. A purely instrumental legal education, or worse, one that prepares its graduates to work with authoritarian regimes and destroys the rule of law and the law itself, would not be fulfilling society's needs. Similarly, a legal education that does not sensitize its graduates toward inequality and or provide them with the knowledge and skills to serve everyone well can produce the effect of exploiting the disadvantaged, deepening inequality, and ultimately leading us to an increasingly unjust world.

NOTES

Chapter I

1. Scaevola (140–82 BC) was a patrician who held the highest magistracies. Servius Sulpicius Rufus (105–43 BC) was also a patrician with a similar cursus honorum. Both Sulpicius and Cicero (106–43 BC) were Scaevola's disciples. Most of Scaevola's work has been lost, but it has come to be known thanks to the commentary of Pomponius and many other great jurists.

2. I translated the French version by Jules Martha, Société d'Édition Les Belles Lettres (Paris, 1923).

3. Of course, there are differences among authorities in dating this period. Jolowicz and Nicholas (1972) differentiate the formative period from the classic period, reducing the latter to the 150 years ending with Ulpian's assassination (AD 232) or the confusion that followed the death of Alexander Severus, but they recognize that most consider a much longer period. Schultz (1946:99), following tradition, makes the period coincide with the Principate, which starts in 27 BC. He points out that the influence of Greek thinking is present in the entirety of Roman history, especially in the last two centuries before Christ, and that the last jurisconsults of the classic period were part of the imperial bureaucracy, which is the main trait of the postclassical or bureaucratic period. Romanists highlight the importance of Scaevola in the intellectual configuration of Roman law, but clearly it was the Principate that produced the greatest number of jurisconsults and that contains all of their most famous work (Domingo, 2004).

4. Atkinson (1970) describes the homes of the prominent jurisconsults, who were nobles of great wealth and power. They had guest rooms and large spaces for gatherings.

5. Roman "clients" were citizens with a special attachment to a paterfamilias.

6. The habit of citing the jurisconsults appeared during the late imperial period (Marotta, 2013).

7. The School of Beirut (Berytus) was established under Septimius Severus's rule at the beginning of the third century. Atkinson (1970) highlights the role of the empress Julia Domma (AD 160–217), a cultured woman interested in law and politics. She was native to what is now Syria. A possible explanation for the school's location is that there were many jurisconsults available in Rome, but Beirut, a Romanized but provincial city, did not have that resource.

8. Pope Honorius III prohibited the teaching of Roman law at the University of Paris at the instigation of the king of France (Koschaker, 1955:125).

9. Jean-Joseph Bugnet, professor between 1822 and 1866 (Huart, 1878).

10. Flaubert (1821–1880) abandoned his law studies and became one of the fundamental writers of French novels in the nineteenth century. His work *Madame Bovary* is a classic of world literature. In a letter of June 25, 1842, he said that the study of law is "embetant" ("boring") and that the law is "killing me, reducing me to an idiot, shattering me" (Le Bos, 2019:164)

11. Ehrlich's best-known work, *Grundlegung der Soziologie des Rechts*, was published in 1913 and had an impact in the United States. Roscoe Pound commented on Ehrlich's contribution in 1922 (Pound, 1922). In 1936, Harvard University Press published the English translation of the *Grundlegung* in the prestigious Harvard Studies in Jurisprudence collection under the title *Fundamental Principles of the Sociology of Law* (Ehrlich, 1936), with a foreword by Pound stressing its importance. Translations into Spanish and Italian had to wait until the end of the twentieth century.

12. Indiano legislation was the Spanish regulation for their American colonies.

13. We will not enter into the discussion of liberalism and its relation with politics, law, and economics in the nineteenth and early twentieth centuries, a particularly complex and controversial field (see Jaksic & Posada Carbó, 2011; Bushnell, 1996; Caballero, 1993; Pérez Perdomo, 1991).

14. The private libraries of intellectuals and professors partially made up for this lack of bibliographical material. The possession of a well-stocked library was (and is) a very important resource and also a sign of distinction of a jurist.

15. Pizani (1909–1997) graduated in Caracas in 1930. In his time, law students had reading and conversation circles that complemented a rather poor education. Pizani later became a professor and, in the 1940s, rector of the

Universidad Central de Venezuela. In 1958–1960, he was minister of education. He was important in promoting the university reform of Córdoba and is recognized for disseminating Kelsen's ideas in Venezuela (personal communication and Pérez Perdomo, 1981).

16. This can be seen in the rapid growth in the number of graduates. For example, in Brazil, there were 15,666 lawyers in 1950 and 85,716 in 1980; in Venezuela, there were 2,087 and 16,045 in the same period. For more countries and data on law students and lawyers, see Pérez Perdomo, 2006.

Chapter II

1. *The Treatise on the Laws of the Realm of England commonly called Glanvill* (1187) and Bracton: *De legibus et consuetunibus Angliae* (c. 1220).

2. Littleton, *Tenures in Englishe* (1576).

3. Fortescue described the education at the Inns of Court during the fifteenth century as follows: "A sort of an Academy, or Gymnasium, fit for persons of their station; where they learn singing, and all kinds of music, dancing and such other accomplishments and diversions . . . At other times, out of term, the greater part apply themselves to the study of the law. Upon festival days, and after the offices of the church are over, they employ themselves to the study of sacred and profane history" (Harno, 1953:6).

4. Edward Coke (1552–1634) was a barrister, parliamentarian, and a judge of enormous importance in English politics. *Institutes of Lawes of England*, in four volumes, is his most important work and was widely used in legal education in the common law, especially in the seventeenth and eighteenth centuries. The first volume was published in 1628 and is the commentary on Littleton. Coke studied at Cambridge and was probably familiar with the civil law tradition.

5. William Blackstone (1723–1780) was an English jurist who graduated as a civil lawyer at Oxford and then became a barrister at the Middle Temple, one of the four traditional Inns of Court. His *Commentaries* was fundamental to the education of jurists in the colonies where it became an authoritative book. It was less successful in England (Prest, 2008).

6. Tocqueville's observation about the political importance of lawyers in the United States was repeated more than a century later by another French observer, Laurent Cohen-Tanugy, but this time comparing the graduates of the most prestigious American law schools with the École Nationale d'Administration, where France educates its political elite. That is why he calls these lawyers the *enarchs* of the United States (Cohen-Tanugi, 1985:37).

7. Matile's interlocutor and the man responsible for the publication of the letter, Édouard de Laboulaye (1811–1883), jurist, writer, and politician, was a remarkable figure. He was a professor at the Collège de France and is one of the

founding fathers of comparative law. Among his numerous works is a history of the United States in three volumes (1855–1866) and *Studies on the Constitution of the United States* (1869). He actively participated in the drafting of the constitution of the Third French Republic and was a senator for life. He is also known as the father of the Statue of Liberty (New York) because he initiated the building project and put effort into it (Gray, 1994).

8. Legal clubs were voluntary associations of students that would discuss, according to their interests, a reading or court decision, or they would receive a guest lecturer. They are no longer called clubs but rather societies or groups and are probably more numerous than in the past. At least in some places, school authorities finance their activities.

9. Amalia Kessler (personal communication) pointed out to me that the realists reacted mainly to rulings of the Supreme Court that annulled much of the social legislation of the time using formalist arguments, but it is also true that the realists were interested in and wrote extensively on legal education.

10. Lawrence Friedman highlights Hurst's personal influence on his career and on what can be called the Wisconsin group (personal conversation with Friedman).

11. I was a student of Fuller's in 1971, when I took a course on law and social change in Africa that made abundant use of anthropological literature that helped students to think about the various means of fulfilling the functions that law performs in modern society. They were interesting and nonthreatening sessions for the students. In that sense, my experience with Fuller was quite different from that of Gordon.

12. The novels are John Jay Osborn's *The Paper Chase* (1971) and Scott Turow's *One L* (1977), both referring to the first year of Harvard Law School. The authors were in fact students, and the professors were easily identifiable. The two novels and the films to which they have given rise were highly critical of the style of various professors and helped to discredit the Socratic method as it was used in most law schools.

13. Luis Bergolla observed to me (personal communication) that law schools can still be very stressful for first-year students and that this has led to the emergence of a coaching and mindfulness industry to help students.

Chapter III

1. There are several networks of lawyers, the largest and best known being Lex Mundi (created in 1989, covering 160 jurisdictions, with 160 members and approximately 21,000 lawyers), World Services Group (created 2003, 141 jurisdictions, 150 members and 19,000 lawyers), and TerraLex (created 1991, 155 jurisdictions, 155 members and 15,000 lawyers). All figures

reported are from 2011. I thank Manuel Gómez for the information about these organizations. (See the website http://www.lawcrossing.com/employers/article/900044704/30-Large-law-firms-networks.)

2. San Tiago Dantas (1911–1964) was one of those intellectual jurists, a law professor in São Paulo, interested in labor law, a novelty for the time, which implied a different conception from traditional civil law. He was also interested in economics and finance and practiced journalism and politics. He was a congressman and minister of foreign affairs and finance in the leftist government of João Goulart (Onofre, 2012; Steiner, 1971).

3. My observations in this section are based on several cases, and those of Dezalay and Garth (2002, 2019) surely on other cases. Neither opinion is based on a collective biography of the professors involved in the educational reforms.

4. Mirjan Damaska (b. 1931) is a Croatian jurist educated in the former Yugoslavia and other European countries, later becoming a professor and dean at the University of Zagreb. Beginning in 1961, he taught periodically at several universities in the United States and is an emeritus professor at Yale. His work in comparative law is highly valued.

5. John H. Merryman (1920–2015) introduced social analysis into comparative law and studied Italian law and legal culture in depth. He appreciated the effort toward change in legal education in Chile, which he knew firsthand as he directed the Stanford program that brought Chilean professors to observe classes and work with Stanford professors. He is well known as a renovator of the comparative law field.

6. Personal information. I was a student in the Harvard master's degree program in 1971.

7. Examples include Harvard Law School: Semester Abroad; International Legal Studies; Stanford Law School: Franke Global Law; Cornell Law School: Semester study abroad program; Northwestern Pritzker School of Law: Study Abroad; Global Opportunities. Since 2012, the Law Schools Global League has brought together universities from around the world, including several from the United States and Latin America.

8. Stewart Macaulay was a student at Stanford in the 1950s. Personal letter on file with the author.

9. Carl Spaeth was dean between 1948 and 1962. He and his successor Bayless Manning (dean from 1964 to 1971) were responsible for transforming a regionally significant law school into one of the leading national institutions (Manning, 2008; Merryman, 2007). During this time, efforts were also made to internationalize the school, which took much longer to bear fruit. Information on the program with India: personal communication from Marc Galanter, who was assistant to the program director. Information on the transformation of

Stanford: interviews with various professors and an oral history series of the law school, as well as the *Stanford Law School Bulletin* and later the *Handbook*.

10. Mauro Cappelletti (1927–2004) was one of the innovators of studies on the civil procedure and justice in Italy and, in general, in Europe. He used comparative methods with great success (Ferrer McGregor, 2009).

REFERENCES

Abbott, Nathan (1901): "The undergraduate study of law." *Annual Report American Bar Association*, 24.

Abel, Richard (1989): *American lawyers*. New York. Oxford University Press.

Abel-Smith, Brian, & R. Stevens (1967): *Lawyers and the courts: A sociological study of English legal system 1750–1965*. London. Heinemann.

Abdulla, Raficq, & M. Keshavjee (2018): *Understanding Sharia: Islamic law in a globalized world*. London. I. B. Tauris.

Alonso Romero, María Paz (2012): *Salamanca, escuela de juristas: Estudios sobre la enseñanza del derecho en el antiguo régimen*. Madrid. Universidad Carlos III.

Ames, James B. (1913): "The vocation of the law professor." In *Lectures in legal history and miscellaneous essays*. Cambridge. Harvard University Press.

Araya Espinoza, Alejandra (2018): "La Facultad de Derecho y su edificio patrimonial: Íconos de la modernidad del siglo XX." A. Araya Espinoza (coord.): *La Facultad de Derecho de la Universidad de Chile: Un nuevo centro para la ciudad*. Santiago. Ediciones del Archivo Central Andrés Bello.

Arnaud, André-Jean (1969): *Les origines doctrinales du Code Civil français*. Paris. Librairie Générale de Droit et Jurisprudence.

Arnaud, André-Jean (1973): *Essai d'analyse structurale du Code Civil français: Les règles du jeu de la paix bourgeoise*. Paris. Librairie Générale de Droit et Jurisprudence.

Arnaud, André-Jean (1975): *Les juristes face à la société du XIXe à nos jours*. Paris. Presses Universitaires de France.

113

Atienza, Soledad (2016): "Moving towards an international legal education in Spain." In C. Jamin & W. van Caenegem, eds., *The internationalization of legal education*. Cham. Springer.

Atkinson, Kathleen (1970): "The education of lawyers in ancient Rome." *South African Law Journal*, 87.

Audren, Frédéric, & J. L. Halpérin (2013): *La culture juridique française: Entre mythes et réalités (XIXᵉ–XXᵉ siècle)*. Paris. CNRS.

Aveledo Coll, Guillermo (2011): *Pro religione et patria: República y religión en la crisis de la Sociedad colonial venezolana (1810–1834)*. Caracas. Universidad Metropolitana y Academia Nacional de la Historia.

Baker, John H. (1984): *The order of serjeants at law*. London. Selden Society

Baker, John H. (1998): "The three languages of the common law." *McGill Law Journal*, 41.

Baker, John H. (2007): *Legal education in London 1250–1850*. London. Selden Society.

Baker, John H. (2012): *The men of court 1440 to 1550: A prosopography of the inns of courts and Chancery and courts of law*. London. Selden Society.

Baker, John H. (2019): *An introduction to English legal history*. 5th ed. Oxford. Oxford University Press.

Barman, Roderick, & J. Barman (1976): "The role of the law graduate in the political elite of imperial Brazil." *Journal of Interamerican Studies and World Affairs*, 18.

Bartie, Susan, & D. Sandomierski, eds. (2021): *American legal education abroad*. New York. New York University Press.

Barton, John H., J. L. Gibbs, V. H. Li, & J. H. Merryman (1983): *Law in radically different cultures*. St. Paul. West Publishing.

Bastos, Aurélio W. (1978): "O estado e a formação dos currículos jurídicos do Brasil." In A. W. Bastos, ed., *Os cursos jurídicos e as elites políticas brasileiras*. Brasília. Câmara dos Deputados.

Bastos, Aurélio W. (2000): *O ensino jurídico no Brasil*. 2nd ed. Rio de Janeiro. Lumen Juris.

Becchi, Paolo (2009): "German legal science: The crisis of natural law theory, the historicisms, and 'conceptual jurisprudence.'" In D. Canale & P. Grossi, eds., *A treatise of legal philosophy and general jurisprudence. Vol 9: A history of the philosophy of law 1600–1900*. Dordrecht. Springer.

Beck Varela, Laura (2013): *Literatura jurídica y censura: Fortuna de Vinnius en España*. Valencia. Tirant lo Blanch y Universidad de Sevilla.

Becker, Marc (2012): "In search of tinterillos." *Latin American Research Review*, 47 (95–114).

Bello, Andrés (1832): *Principios de derecho de jentes*. Santiago, Chile. Imprenta de la Opinión.

Bello, Andrés (1843): *Discurso pronunciado en la instalación de la Universidad de Chile el día 13 de septiembre de 1843* (uchile.cl/portal/presentación/historia/4682/ dicursoinaugural).

Bernstein, Richard B. (2004): *Thomas Jefferson: The revolution of ideas*. New York. Oxford University Press.

Bogdan, Michael (2013): *Concise introduction to comparative law*. Groningen. Europa Law Publishing.

Bréhier, Louis (1926): "Notes sur l'histoire de l'enseignement supérieur à Constantinople." *Byzantion*, 3.

Brown, Brendan F. (1961): "Recent significant trends in legal education in the Americas." *Inter-American Law Review*, 55.

Brundage, James A. (2008): *The medieval origins of the legal profession: Canonists, civilians and courts*. Chicago. University of Chicago Press.

Brutti, Mario (2011): "Vittorio Scialoja: Diritto romano e sistema nel tardo ottocento." *Bullettino dell'Istituto de Diritto Romano Vittorio Scialoja*, 105.

Burrage, Michael (1996): "From gentlemen's to public profession: Status and politics in the history of English solicitors." *International Journal of the legal profession*, 3.

Burkholder, Mark, & D. Chandler (1977): *From impotence to authority: The Spanish crown and the audiencias, 1687-1808*. Columbia. University of Missouri Press.

Bushnell, David (1996): "Assessing the legacy of liberalism." In V. Peloso & B. Tenebaum, eds., *Liberals, politics and power: State formation in nineteenth century Latin America*. Athens. University of Georgia Press.

Caballero, Manuel (1993): *Gómez, el tirano liberal: Vida y muerte del siglo XIX*. Caracas. Monte Ávila Editores.

Calasso, Francesco (1954): *Medio evo del diritto*. Milan. Giuffrè.

Câmara dos Deputados (1977): *Criação dos cursos jurídicos no Brasil*. Brasília. Fundação Rui Barbosa.

Caroni, Pio (2013): *Lecciones de historia de la codificación*. Madrid. Universidad Carlos III.

Cappelletti, Mauro, & B. Garth, eds. (1978–1979): *Access to justice*. Alpheenendenrijn. Sithoff and Noordhoff.

Capriles, Victoria, & R. Pérez Perdomo (2019): "Los abogados graduados en la Universidad Metropolitana de Caracas 2006–2016: Estudio de una cohorte profesional en tiempos de revolución." *Pedagogía Universitaria y Didáctica del Derecho*, 6.

Chase, Anthony (1979): "The birth of the modern law school." *American Journal of Legal History*, 23.

Chroust, Anton-Hermann (1954): "Legal education in ancient Rome." *Journal of Legal Education*, 7.

Chroust, Anton-Hermann (1965): *The rise of the legal profession in America.* Norman. University of Oklahoma Press.

Cicero, Marco T: *Brutus.* Paris. Société d'Édition Les Belles Lettres, 1923.

Clark, David S. (1998): "Transnational legal practice: The need for global law schools." *American Journal of Comparative Law*, 46.

Clark, David S. (2012): "Legal education." In D. S. Clark, ed., *Comparative law and society.* Cheltenham. Edward Elgar.

Cohen-Tanugi, Laurent (1985): *Le droit sans l'état: Sur la démocratie en France et en Amérique.* Paris. Presses Universitaires de France.

Coing, Helmut (1959): *Historia y significado de la idea del sistema en la jurisprudencia.* Mexico City. Universidad Nacional Autónoma de México.

Coing, Helmut (1977): "Las facultades de leyes de la ilustración europea." *Anales Valentinos*, 3, no. 6.

Colmo, Alfredo (1915): *La cultura jurídica y la facultad de derecho.* Buenos Aires. Martín García.

Coppola, Sophia, writer and dir. (2003): *Lost in translation.* Focus Features.

Coquillette, Daniel R., & B. Kimball (2015): *On the battlefield of merit: Harvard Law School, the first century.* Cambridge. Harvard University Press.

Cownie, Fiona (1999): "Searching for theory in teaching law." In F. Cownie, ed., *The law school: Global issues, local questions.* Aldershot. Ashgate Dartmouth.

Curzon, Alfred de (1919): "L'enseignement du droit français dans les universités de France aux XVIIᵉ et XVIIIᵉ siècles." *Nouvelle Revue Historique de Droit Français et Étranger*, 43.

Damaska, Mirjan (1968): "A continental lawyer in an American law school: Trials and tribulations of adjustment." *University of Pennsylvania Law Review*, 8.

Dantas, San Tiago (1955): "A educação jurídica e a crise politica brasileira." *Revista Forense*, 59.

David, René (1964): *Les grands systèmes de droit contemporains.* Paris. Sirey.

David, René (1965): *Le droit anglais.* Paris. Presses Universitaires de France.

Dezalay, Yves, & B. Garth (2002): *The internationalization of palace wars: Lawyers, economists, and the context to transform Latin American states.* Chicago. University of Chicago Press.

Dezalay, Yves, & B. Garth (2021): *Law as reproduction and revolution. An interconnected history.* Oakland. University of California Press.

Dicey, Albert V. (1883): *Can English law be taught at the universities? An inaugural lecture delivered at All Souls College, 21st April, 1883.* London. Macmillan and Co.

Dicey, Albert V. (1900): "The teaching of English law at Harvard." *Harvard Law Review*, 13, 422.

Domat, Jean (1689): *Les loix civiles dans leur ordre naturel*. Paris. Jean Jacques Coignard, Imprimeur du Roi.

Domingo, Rafael (2004): "La jurisprudencia romana, cuna del derecho." *Anales de la Real Academia de Ciencias Morales y Políticas*, 81.

Ehrlich, Eugen (1936): *Fundamental principles of the sociology of law*. Cambridge. Harvard University Press.

Eisenmann, Charles (1954): *Les sciences sociales dans l'enseignement supérieur. Droit*. Paris. UNESCO.

Elliott, J. H. (2006): *Empires of the Atlantic world: Britain and Spain in America 1492–1830*. New Haven. Yale University Press.

Evêque, Ralph (2019): "La diffusion du savoir juridique à Rome. De la transmission pratique du droit à l'émergence d'un ensignement académique." In M. Cavina (a cura de): *L'insegnamento del diritto (secoli XII–XX)*. Bologna. Il Mulino.

Falcão, Joaquim (1978): "Os cursos jurídicos e a formação do estado nacional." In A. W. Bastos, ed., *Os cursos jurídicos e as elites políticas brasileiras*. Brasília. Câmara dos Deputados.

Falcão, Joaquim (1979): "Lawyers in Brazil: Ideals and praxis." *International Journal of the Sociology of Law*, 7.

Falcão, Joaquim (1984): *Os advogados. Ensino jurídico e mercado de trabalho*. Recife. Fundação Joaquim Nabuco y Editora Massangana.

Febres Cordero, Foción (1959): *Reforma universitaria*. Caracas. Universidad Central del Venezuela.

Feldman, Stephen M. (2004): "The transformation of an academic discipline: Law professors in the past and future (or Toy Story too)." *Journal of Legal Education*, 54.

Ferling, John (1993): *John Adams: A life*. New York. Oxford University Press.

Ferrer Mac-Gregor, Eduardo (2009): "Mauro Cappelletti y el derecho procesal constitucional comparado." *Anuario Iberoamericano de Justicia Constitucional*, 13.

Fisher, William (2006): "Oliver Wendell Holmes." In D. Kennedy & W. Fisher, eds., *The canon of American legal thought*. Princeton. Princeton University Press.

Fix-Zamudio, Héctor (1976): "En torno a los problemas de la metodología del derecho." In J. Witker, comp., *Antología de estudios sobre la enseñanza del derecho*. Mexico City. Universidad Nacional Autónoma de México.

Frank, Jerome (1931): *Law and the modern mind*. New York. Brentano.

Frier, Bruce W. (1985): *The rise of Roman jurists: Studies on Cicero's Pro-Caecina*. Princeton. Princeton University Press.

Friedman, Lawrence M. (1973): *A history of American law*. New York. Simon & Schuster.

Friedman, Lawrence M. (2001): "Erewhon: The coming legal order." *Stanford Journal for International Law*, 37.

Friedman, Lawrence M. (2002): *American law in the 20th century*. New Haven. Yale University Press.

Friedman, Lawrence (2011): *The human rights culture. A study in history and context*. New Orleans. Quid Pro Books.

Fuller, Lon L. (1948): "What the law school can contribute to the making of lawyers." *Journal of Legal Education*, 1.

Fuller, Lon L. (1950): "On teaching law." *Stanford Law Review*, 3.

Fuller, Lon L. (1961): *El caso de los exploradores de cavernas*. Buenos Aires. Abeledo Perrot.

Gaitán Bohórquez, Julio (2002): *Huestes de estado: La formación universitaria de los juristas en los comienzos del estado colombiano*. Bogotá. Centro Editorial de la Universidad del Rosario.

García Chuecos, Héctor (1937): *Estudios de historia colonial venezolana*. Caracas. Tipografía Americana.

García Gallo, Alfonso (1977): "La ciencia jurídica en la formación del derecho hispanoamericano de los siglos XVI al XVIII." *La formazione storica del diritto moderno in Europa: Atti del terzo congresso Internazionale della società italiana di storia del diritto*. Florence. Leo Olschki.

García Gallo, Alfonso (1997): *Atlas histórico jurídico*. Mexico City. UNAM and Porrúa.

García La Guardia, Jorge M. (1976): "La universidad latinoamericana y la formación de los juristas." In J. Witker, ed., *Antología de estudios sobre la enseñanza del derecho*. Mexico City. Universidad Nacional Autónoma de México.

García Pelayo, Manuel (1962): "La idea medieval del derecho." *Revista de la Facultad de Derecho de la Universidad Central de Venezuela*, 23.

García Pelayo, Manuel (1969): "Auctoritas." *Revista de la Facultad de Derecho de la Universidad Central de Venezuela*, 42.

Gardner, James A. (1980): *Legal imperialism: American lawyers and foreign aid in Latin America*. Madison. University of Wisconsin Press.

Garth, Bryant, & G. Schaffer (2022): "The globalization of legal education: A critical perspective." In B. Garth & G. Schaffer, eds., *The globalization of legal education: A critical perspective*. Oxford. Oxford University Press.

Gény, François (1899): *Méthode d'interprétation et sources en droit privé positif*. Paris. Librairie Générale de Droit et de Jurisprudence.

Ghirardi, José G. (2021): "Legal teaching and the reconceptualization of the state: Global law and the new legal education." In S. Bartie & D. Sandomierski, eds., *American legal education abroad*. New York. New York University Press.

Giddens, Anthony (2000): *Runaway world: How globalization is shaping our lives*. New York. Routledge.

Gigandel, Cyrille (1991): "George Auguste Matile." *Dictionnaire historique de la Suisse*. Bern. Rohr.

Gil Fortoul, José (1956): *Obras completas, vol. 5: El humo de mi pipa*. Caracas. Ministerio de Educación.

Gilmore, Grant (1977): *Ages of American law*. New Haven. Yale University Press.

Giner de los Ríos, Francisco (1889/2003): "Sobre la reorganización de los estudios de la facultad." In F. J. Laporta, ed., *La enseñanza del derecho*. Madrid. Universidad Autónoma de Madrid y Boletín Oficial del Estado.

Glendon, M. A., P. Carozza, & C. Picker (2008): *Comparative legal traditions in a nutshell*. St. Paul. Thomson West.

Goebel, Julius, Jr. (1955): *A history of the School of Law, Columbia University*. New York. Columbia University Press.

Gómez, Manuel A. (2003): "Los abogados de negocios en Venezuela." *Revista de la Facultad de Ciencias Jurídicas y Políticas de la Universidad Central de Venezuela*, 125.

Gómez, Manuel A. (2018): "Innovaciones en la educación jurídica latinoamericana y políticas públicas en tiempos de globalización." In G. González Mantilla, ed., *La educación jurídica como política pública en América Latina*. Lima. Palestra Editores.

Gómez, Manuel A., & R. Pérez Perdomo (2018): *Big law in Latin America and Spain: Globalization and adjustments in the provision of high-end legal services*. London. Palgrave Macmillan.

Gómez, Manuel A., & M. Galanter (2020): "The many lives of big law: Three decades in the evolution of large law firms." In R. Abel, H. Sommerlad, O. Hammersley, & U. Schultz, eds., *Lawyers in society*. Vol. 2.

Gómez, Manuel A. (2021): "Beyond borders and across legal traditions: The transnationalization of Latin American lawyers." In P. Zumbansen, ed., *The Oxford handbook of transnational law*. New York. Oxford University Press.

González, Florentino (1871): *Lecciones de derecho constitucional*. 2nd ed. Paris. Rosa y Buret.

Gonzales Mantilla, Gorki (2008): *La enseñanza del derecho o los molinos de viento: Cambios, resistencias y continuidades*. Lima. Pontificia Universidad Católica del Perú and Palestra.

González Mantilla, Gorki, ed. (2018): *La educación jurídica como política pública en América Latina*. Lima. Palestra Editores.

Gordon, Robert W. (1983): "Legal thought and legal practice in the age of American enterprise 1870–1920." In G. L. Geison, ed., *Professions and professional ideologies in America*. Chapel Hill. University of North Carolina.

Gordon, Robert W. (1989): "Critical legal studies as a teaching method." *Legal Education Review*, 1.

Gordon, Robert W. (1995). "The case for (and against) Harvard." *Michigan Law Review*, 93, no. 6.

Gordon, Robert W. (2004): "Professors and policy makers: Yale law faculty in the New Deal and after." In A. T. Kronan, ed., *History of the Yale Law School: The tercentennial lectures*. New Haven. Yale University Press.

Gordon, Robert W. (2007): "The geological strata of the law school curriculum." *Vanderbilt Law Review*, 60.

Gray, John C. (1908): *Select cases and other authorities on the law of property*. Cambridge. George H. Kent.

Gray, Walter D. (1994): *Interpreting American democracy in France: The career of Édouard de Laboulaye 1811–1883*. Newark. University of Delaware Press.

Grey, Thomas C. (1983): "Langdell's orthodoxy." *University of Pittsburgh Law School*, 45.

Grossi, Paolo (1986): *Stile fiorentino: Gli studi giuridici nella Firenze italiana 1859–1950*. Milan. Giuffrè.

Grossi, Paolo (2000): *Scienza giuridica italiana: Un profilo storico 1860–1950*. Milan. Giuffrè.

Grossi, Paolo (2010): *A history of European law*. Chichester. Wiley-Blackwell.

Gualazzini, Ugo (1974): *L'insegnamento del diritto in Italia durante l'alto Medioevo*. Mediolani. Typis, Giuffrè.

Guzmán Brito, Alejandro (1982): *Andrés Bello codificador: Historia de la fijación y codificación del derecho civil en Chile*. Santiago. Universidad de Chile.

Guzmán Brito, Alejandro (2000): *La codificación civil en Iberoamérica: Siglos XIX y XX*. Santiago. Editorial Jurídica de Chile.

Hakim, Nader (2005): "La contribution de l'université à l'élaboration de la doctrine civiliste au XIXᵉ siècle." In M. Hecquard-Théron, *Les facultés de droit inspiratrices du droit?* Toulouse. Presses de l'Université Toulouse 1 Capitole.

Halpérin, Jean-Louis (1992): *L'impossible code civil*. Paris. Presses Universitaires de France.

Halpérin, Jean-Louis (2007): "Bugnet, Jean-Joseph." *Dictionnaire historique des juristes français: XIIᵉ–XXᵉ siècle*. Paris. Presses Universitaires de France.

Halpérin, Jean-Louis (2009): "French legal science in the 17th and 18th centuries: To the limits of the theory of law." In D. Canale and P. Grossi, eds., *A treatise of legal philosophy and general jurisprudence. Vol. 9: A history of the philoso-phy of law in the civil law world.* New York. Springer.

Halpérin, Jean-Louis, ed. (2011): *Paris, capitale juridique (1804–1950): Étude de socio-histoire sur la faculté de droit de Paris.* Paris. Éditions Rue d'Ulm.

Halpérin, Jean-Louis (2015): *Histoire de l'état des juristes: Allemagne XIXᵉ–XXᵉ siècle.* Paris. Garnier.

Halpérin, Jean-Louis (2021): "Legal education in France turns its attention to the Harvard model." In S. Bartie & D. Sandomierski, eds., *American legal education abroad.* New York. New York University Press.

Hanbury, Harold G. (1958): *The Vinerian chair and legal education.* Oxford. Basil Blackwell.

Hannisch Espíndola, Hugo (1981): "Fuentes de 'Instituciones de Derecho Romano' compuestas por Andrés Bello y publicadas sin nombre de autor." *Bello y Chile: Tercer congreso del bicentenario.* Caracas. La Casa de Bello.

Harno, Albert J. (1953): *Legal education in the United States: A report prepared for the survey of the legal profession.* San Francisco. Bancroft-Whitney.

Hawkins, Hugh (1972): *Between Harvard and America: The educational leadership of Charles W. Eliot.* New York. Oxford University Press.

Heringa, Aalt W. (2011): "European legal education: The Maastricht experi-ence." *Penn State International Law Review,* 29.

Herzog, Tamar (2018): *A short history of European law: The last two and half millen-nia.* Cambridge. Harvard University Press.

Holmes, Oliver (1880): "Book notices: Langdell and Anson on contract." *Ameri-can Law Review,* 14.

Holmes, Oliver W. (1897): *The path of the law.* In D. Kennedy & W. W. Fisher III, eds., *The canon of American legal thought.* Princeton. Princeton University Press. 2006.

Hotman, François (1567): *Antitriboniano o discurso de un grande y reputado juriscon-sulto de nuestro tiempo sobre el estudio de las leyes.* Bilingual edition. Madrid. Universidad Carlos III. 2013.

Howley, Joseph A. (2013): "Why read the jurists? Aulus Gellius on reading across disciplines." In P. du Plessis, *Law and society in the Roman world.* Edinburgh. Edinburgh University Press.

Huart, A. (1878): "Notice sur M. Bugnet, Professeur de Code Civil à la Faculté de Paris (1822–1866)." *Nouvelle Revue Historique de Droit Français et Étranger,* 2.

Huffcut, Ernest W. (1902): "A decade of progress in legal education." *American Lawyer,* 10, 404–409.

Hull, N. E. H. (1995): "Vital school of jurisprudence: Roscoe Pound, Wesley Newcomb Hohfeld, and the promotion of academic jurisprudence agenda." *Journal of Legal Education,* 45, 235–283.

Hurst, James W. (1950): *The growth of American law: The law makers.* Boston. Little Brown.

Hurst, James W. (1956): *Law and the conditions of freedom in nineteenth century United States.* Madison. University of Wisconsin Press.

Jamin, Cristophe (2011): "Le droit des manuels de droit ou l'art de traiter la moitié du sujet." In A. S. Chambost, *Histoire des manuels de droit.* Paris. Librairie Générale de Droit et Jurisprudence.

Jamin, Christophe (2012): *La cuisine du droit. L'École de Droit de Sciences Po: Une expérience française.* Paris. LGDJ/Lextenso éditions.

Jamin, Christophe, & W. van Caenegem (2016): "The internationalization of legal education: General report of the Vienna congress of the International Academy of Comparative Law." In C. Jamin & W. van Caenegem, eds., *The internationalization of legal education.* Cham. Springer.

Jaksic, Iván, & E. Posada Carbó (2011): "Introducción: Naufragios y sobrevivencia del liberalismo latinoamericano." In I. Jaksic & E. Posada Carbó, eds., *Liberalismo y poder: Latinoamérica en el siglo XIX.* Mexico City. Fondo de Cultura Económica.

Jhering, Rudolf von (1976): *La lucha por el derecho.* 1872. Madrid. Doncel.

Jolowicz, Herbert F., & B. Nicholas (1972): *Historical introduction to the study of Roman Law.* Cambridge. Cambridge University Press.

Kalman, Laura (1986): *Legal realism at Yale 1927-1960.* Chapel Hill. University of North Carolina Press.

Kalman, Laura (2005): *Yale Law School and the sixties: Revolt and reverberations.* Chapel Hill. University of North Carolina Press.

Kalman, Mark G. (1987): *A guide to critical legal studies.* Cambridge. Harvard University Press.

Kennedy, David, & W. W. Fisher III, eds. (2006): *The canon of American legal thought.* Princeton. Princeton University Press.

Kennedy, Duncan (1970-71). "How the law school fails: A polemic." *Yale Review of Law and Social Action,* 1.

Kennedy, Duncan, ed. (2004): *Legal education and the reproduction hierarchy: A polemic against the system.* New York. New York University Press.

Kimball, Bruce A. (2004): "The Langdell problem: Historicizing the century of historiography 1906-2000s." *Law and History Review,* 22.

Kimball, Bruce A. (2006): "The proliferation of case method teaching in American law schools: Mr. Langdell's emblematic 'abomination,' 1890-1915." *History of Education Quarterly,* 46, no. 2.

Kimball, Bruce A. (2009): *The inception of modern professional education: C. C. Langdell, 1826-1909.* Chapel Hill. University of North Carolina Press.

Kimball, Bruce, & D. R. Coquillette (2020): *The intellectual sword: Harvard Law School, the second century.* Cambridge. Harvard University Press.

Kimball, Bruce A. (2021): "The proliferation and transformation of Harvard case method in the United States, 1870–1990s." In S. Bartie & D. Sandomierski, eds., *American legal education abroad.* New York. New York University Press.

Konig, David T. (2012): "Thomas Jefferson and the practice of law." *Encyclopedia Virginia.* Charlottesville. Virginia Foundation for the Humanities.

Koschaker, Pablo (1955): *Europa y el derecho romano.* Madrid. Editorial Revista de Derecho Privado.

Kuskowski, Ada M. (2022): *Vernacular law: Writing and reinvention of customary law in medieval France.* Cambridge. Cambridge University Press.

Langbein, John H. (2004a): "Blackstone, Lichtfield and Yale: The founding of Yale Law School." In A. T. Kronman, ed., *History of the Yale Law School: The tercentennial lectures.* New Haven. Yale University Press.

Langbein, John H. (2004b): "Law school in a university: Yale distinctive path in the late nineteenth century." In A. T. Kronman, ed., *History of the Yale Law School: The tercentennial lectures.* New Haven. Yale University Press.

Langbein, J. H., R. L. Lerner, & B. P. Smith, eds. (2009): *History of the common law. The development of Anglo-American legal institutions.* Austin. Wolters Kluwers.

Langdell, Christopher Columbus (1993); "Harvard celebration speech." 1887. *Law Quarterly Review*, 3. In Martin L. Levine, ed., *Legal education.* New York. New York University Press.

LaPiana, William P. (1994): *Logic and experience: The origins of modern American legal education.* New York. Oxford University Press.

Lasswell, Harold, & M. McDougal (1943): "Legal education and public policy: Professional training in the public interest." *Yale Law Journal*, 52.

Lawson, Frederick H. (1968): *The Oxford Law School 1850–1968.* Oxford. Clarendon Press.

Lazarus-Black, Mindie, & J. Globokar (2015): "Foreign attorneys in US LL.M. programs: Who's in, who's out and who they are." *Indiana Journal of Global Legal Studies*, 22, 3.

Lazarus-Black, Mindie (2017): "The voice of the stranger: Foreign LL.M. students' experience of culture, law and pedagogy in US law schools." In J. A. R. Nafziger, ed., *Comparative law and anthropology.* Cheltenham. Edward Elgar.

Leal, Ildefonso (1963): *Historia de la Universidad de Caracas. 1721–1827.* Caracas. Universidad Central de Venezuela.

Leal, Ildefonso (1978): *Los estatutos republicanos de la Universidad Central de Venezuela 1827.* Caracas. Universidad Central de Venezuela.

Le Bos, Yves-Edouard (2019): "L'enseignement du droit par 'École de l'exégèse.' Pourquoi tant d'ennui sur les bancs de l'université." In M. Carvina, *L'insegnamento del diritto (secoli XII-XX)*. Bologna. Il Mulino.

Le Goff, Jacques (1985): *Les intellectuels au Moyen Age*. Paris. Seuil.

Lempert, David (2003): "After five decades: Stanford Law School class of 1952." *Legal Studies Forum*, 27, 265–275.

Lesaffer, Randall (2009): *European legal history: A cultural and political perspective*. Cambridge. Cambridge University Press.

Levack, Brian (1973): *The civil lawyers in England, 1603–1641: A political study*. Clarendon Press. Oxford.

Levine, Martin L., ed. (1993): *Legal education*. New York. New York University Press.

Lévêque, François (1918): "Alfredo Colmo: La cultura jurídica de las facultades de derecho." *Revue Internationale de l'Enseignement*, 72.

Lewin, Bolislao (1942): *Los León Pinelo; la ilustre familia marrana del siglo XVII ligada a la historia de Argentina, Perú, América y España*. Buenos Aires. Sociedad Hebraica Argentina.

Li, Xiaping (1999): "La civilisation chinoise et son droit." *Revue Internationale de Droit Comparé*, 3.

Lista, Carlos A., & A. N. Brígido (2002): *La enseñanza del derecho y la formación de la conciencia jurídica*. Córdoba. Sima Editores.

Llewellyn, Karl N. (1930): *The bramble bush: Lectures on law and its study*. New York. Columbia Law School.

Llewellyn, Karl N. (1935): "On what is wrong with so-called legal education." *Columbia Law Review*, 35.

López Villaverde, Ángel L (2021): *80 años del exilio de los españoles acogidos en México*. Tirant lo Blanch.

Lynch, Dennis O. (1981): *Legal roles in Colombia*. Uppsala. Scandinavian Institute for African Studies. New York. International Center for Law in Development.

Macaulay, Stewart (2003): *Contracts: Law in action*. 2nd ed. Newark. LexisNexis.

Mago de Chópite, Lila (1997): "La población de Caracas (1754–1820): Estructura y características." *Anuario de Estudios Americanos*, 54.

Malatesta, María (2011): "Italian legal elites: The classical model and its transformation." In Yves Dezalay & B. Garth, eds., *Lawyers and the rule of law in an era of globalization*. New York. Routledge.

Manning, Bayless (2008): *Bayless Manning: Reflections on his years at Stanford Law School*. Interviewed by Sarah F. Wilson, Feb. 18, 2008. Oral History Series, Stanford Law School.

Maravall, Juan Antonio (1972): *Estado moderno y mentalidad social*. Madrid. Ediciones de la Revista de Occidente.

Marotta, Valerio (2013): "La *recitatio* degli scritti giurisprudenziali: Premessa repubblicana e alto imperiale di una prassi tardo antica." In V. Marotta & E. Stolfi, *Ius controversum e processo fra tarda repubblica ed età dei Severi.* Roma. L'Erma di Bretschneider.

Marrou, Henri I. (1981): *Histoire de l'éducation dans l'antiquité.* 7th ed. Paris. Éditions du Seuil.

Martin Frechilla, Juan José (2006): *Forja y crisol. La Universidad Central de Venezuela y los exiliados de la guerra civil española.* Caracas. Universidad Central de Venezuela.

Martínez Garnica, Armando (2019): *Historia de la Primera República de Colombia, 1819–1831.* Bogotá. Universidad del Rosario.

Martínez Paz, Enrique (1913): *La enseñanza del derecho en la Universidad de Córdoba.* Córdoba.

Martínez Tapia, Ramón (1996): "Leibniz y la ciencia jurídica." *Anales de Derecho: Universidad de Murcia.* 14.

Matile, George A. (1864): *Les écoles de droit aux États-Unis: Lettre adressée à M. Edouard Laboulaye, professeur au Collège de France.* Paris.

Mattingly, Paul H. (2017): *American academic cultures: A history of higher education.* Chicago. Chicago University Press.

McDougal, Myres S. (1947): "The law school of the future: From legal realism to policy science in the world community." *Yale Law Journal,* 56.

McKenna, Marian (1986): *Tapping Reeve and the Litchfield Law School.* New York. Oceana. 1986.

Melich Orsini, José (1976): "La ciencia del derecho en el último siglo: Venezuela." In M. Rotondi, ed., *La science du droit au cours du dernier siècle.* Padua. Antonio Milani.

Meneses Reyes, Rodrigo (2018): "Lawyering in the margins: Lawyers and drug criminals before Mexican courts." *International Journal of the Legal Profession,* 25.

Merryman, John H. (1974): "Legal education there and here: A comparison" *Stanford Law Review,* 27.

Merryman, J. H., D. S. Clark, & L. M. Friedman, eds. (1979): *Law and social change in Mediterranean Europe and Latin America: A handbook of legal and social indicators for comparative law study.* Stanford. Stanford Law School. New York. Dobbs Ferry.

Merryman, John Henry (2000a): "Law and development memoirs I: The Chile law program" *American Journal of Comparative Law,* 48.

Merryman, John Henry (2000b): "Law and development memoirs II: Slade." *American Journal of Comparative Law,* 48, 713.

Merryman, John Henry (2007): *The John Merryman story*. Stanford Law School Library.

Merryman, John H., & R. Pérez Perdomo (2019): *The civil law tradition*. 4th ed. Stanford. Stanford University Press.

Mertz, Elizabeth (2007): *The language of the law school: Learning to "think like a lawyer."* Oxford. Oxford University Press.

Mijares, Augusto (1953): "Prólogo." In Juan Germán Roscio, *Obras completas*, vol. 1. Caracas. Secretaría Décima Conferencia Interamericana.

Miliani, Domingo (1983): "Prólogo." In Juan Germán Roscio, *El triunfo de la libertad sobre el despotismo*. Caracas. Monte Ávila.

Moccia, Luigi (1988): "Il legislatore del 'diritto comune' continentale (secolo XVI-XVIII) nell'opera de Gino Gorla." In A. Giuliani & N. Picardi, *L'educazione giuridica: Modelli di legislatore e scienza del la legislazione*. Perugia. Edizione Scientifiche Italiane.

Moline, Brian J. (2002): "Early American legal education." *Washburn Law Journal*, 42, 775.

Monheit, Michael I. (1997): "Guillaume Bude, Andrea Alciato, Pierre de l'Estoile: Renaissance interpreters of Roman law." *Journal of History of Ideas*, 58.

Morley, Godfrey (1975): "Legal education in England and Wales." In A. Giuliani & N. Picardi, *L'Educazione giuridica. Modelli di università e progetti di riforma*. Perugia. Libreria Universitaria.

Mouchet, Carlos (1960): "Florentino González, un jurista de América: Sus ideas sobre el régimen municipal." *Journal of Inter-American Studies*, 2, no. 1.

Novísimos estatutos de esta Universidad Central de Venezuela (1827). Published as *Los estatutos republicanos de la Universidad Central de Venezuela 1827*. Caracas. Universidad Central del Venezuela, 1978.

Onofre, Gabriel da Fonseca (2012): *Em busca da esquerda esquecida: San Tiago Dantas e o frente progessista*. Rio de Janeiro. Mestrado em Histoia, Politica e Bens Culturais, Fundaçao Getulio Vargas.

Ortiz, Tulio (2015): "Los profesores de la Facultad de Derecho y Ciencias Sociales en tiempos del primer peronismo y otros temas conexos." In T. Ortiz, ed., *Facultad de Derecho y Ciencias Sociales: Enseñanzas de su historia*. Buenos Aires. Universidad de Buenos Aires.

Osborn, John Jay (1971): *The paper chase*. Boston. Houghton Mifflin.

Packer, Herbert, & T. Ehrlich (1972): *New directions in legal education*. New York. McGraw-Hill.

Padoa-Schioppa, Antonio (2017): *A history of law in Europe from early Middle Ages to the twentieth century*. Cambridge. Cambridge University Press.

Paricio, Javier (2018): *Respondere ex auctoritate principis. Eficacia de las respuestas de los juristas en la experiencia jurídica romana*. Madrid. Marcial Pons.

Parra Márquez, Héctor (1952): *Historia del Colegio de Abogados de Caracas.* Tomo Primero. Caracas. Imprenta Nacional.

Pérez Collados, José M., & S. R. Barbosa, eds. (2012): *Juristas de la independencia.* Madrid. Marcial Pons.

Pérez Godoy, Fernando (2015): "La teoría del derecho natural y de gentes de Johannes Heineccius en la cultura jurídica iberoamericana." *Revista de Estudios Histórico-jurídicos*, 37.

Pérez Hurtado, Luis F. (2009): *La futura generación de abogados mexicanos. Estudio de las escuelas y los estudiantes de derecho en México.* Mexico City. Centro de Estudios sobre la Enseñanza y el Aprendizaje de Derecho and Universidad Nacional Autónoma de México.

Pérez Lledó, Juan A. (1996): *El movimiento critical legal studies.* Madrid. Tecnos.

Pérez Lledó, Juan A. (2003): "Teoría y práctica de la enseñanza del derecho." En F. J. Laporta, ed., *La enseñanza del derecho.* Madrid. Universidad Autónoma de Madrid y Boletín Oficial del Estado.

Pérez Perdomo, Rogelio (1974): *Tres ensayos sobre los métodos de la educación jurídica.* Caracas. Universidad Central de Venezuela.

Pérez Perdomo, Rogelio (1975): "Le discours du professeur comme modèle de raisonnement juridique." In A. Giuliani, *Educazione giuridica.* Perugia. Librería Universitaria.

Pérez Perdomo, Rogelio (1981): *Los abogados en Venezuela, estudio de una élite intelectual y política 1780–1980.* Caracas. Monte Ávila.

Pérez Perdomo, Rogelio (1988): "Teoría y práctica de la legislación en la temprana República (Venezuela 1821–1870)." In A. Giuliani & N. Picardi, *L'educazione giuridica. Modelli di legislatore e scienza del la legislazione.* Perugia. Edizione Scientifiche Italiane.

Pérez Perdomo, Rogelio (1991): "Liberalismo y derecho en el siglo XIX de América Latina." *Sociologia del Diritto*, 19, no. 2.

Pérez Perdomo, Rogelio (2001): "Oil lawyers and the globalization of Venezuelan oil industry." In R. Appelbaum, W. Felstiner, & V. Gessner, eds., *Rules and networks: The legal culture of global legal transactions.* Oxford. Hart.

Pérez-Perdomo, Rogelio (2006): *Latin American lawyers: A historical introduction.* Stanford. Stanford University Press.

Pérez Perdomo, Rogelio (2012): "Héctor Fix-Zamudio y la investigación profesional en el derecho." *Revista de la Facultad de Ciencias Jurídicas y Políticas: Universidad Central de Venezuela*, 136.

Pérez Perdomo, Rogelio (2018): "Educación jurídica y política en Venezuela revolucionaria." In G. González Mantilla, ed., *La educación jurídica como política pública en América Latina.* Lima. Palestra Editores.

Pérez Perdomo, Rogelio (2019): "Lost in translation? Latin American lawyers-students in American law schools. Transplants and globalization." *Oñati Socio Legal Series*, 9.

Pérez-Perdomo, Rogelio (2020): "Juan Germán Roscio. Equality and freedom in early 19th century Venezuela." In R. Domingo & M. Mirow, eds., *Law and the Christian tradition of Latin American: Biographies.* London. Routledge.

Pérez-Perdomo, Rogelio (2020b): "Abogados golondrinas o la internacionalización de la profesión jurídica: El caso de Venezuela." *Revista Latinoamericana de Sociología del Derecho*, 1.

Pérez Perdomo, Rogelio, & M. A. Gómez (2008): "Innovaciones en la educación jurídica de América Latina." *Derecho y Democracia*, 1.

Peset, Mariano, & M. P. Alonso Romero (2018): "Las facultades de leyes." In L. E. Rodríguez-San Pedro Bezares, ed., *Historia de la Universidad de Salamanca. Vol. 3: Saberes y confluencias.* Salamanca. Ediciones de la Universidad de Salamanca.

Pestalardo, Agustín (1914): *Historia de la enseñanza de las ciencias jurídicas y sociales en la Universidad de Buenos Aires.* Buenos Aires. Imprenta Alsina.

Piano Mortari, Vincenzo (1976): *Dogmatica e interpretazione: I giuristi medievali.* Naples. Jovene Editore.

Piano Mortari, Vincenzo (1978): *Diritto logica metodo nel secolo XVI.* Naples. Jovene Editore.

Platsas, Antonios, & D. Marrani (2016): "On the evolving and dynamic nature of UK legal education." In C. Jamin & W. van Caenegem, eds., *The internationalization of legal education.* Cham. Springer.

Portalis, Jean-Étienne (1801): *Discours préliminaire du premier projet du Code Civil.* (http://bibliotheque.uqac.ca).

Posner, Richard, ed. (1992): *The essential Holmes.* Chicago. University of Chicago Press.

Pothier, Robert Joseph, with J. J. Bugnet (1845): *Œuvres de Pothier annotées et mises en corrélation avec le code civil y la législation actuelle.* Paris. Cosse et N. Delamottes.

Pound, Roscoe (1912): "Social problems and the law." *American Journal of Sociology*, 18.

Pound, Roscoe (1922): "An appreciation of Eugen Ehrlich." *Harvard Law Review*, 36.

Pound, Roscoe (1951): "Some comments on law teachers and law teaching." *Journal of Legal Education*, 3.

Prest, Wilfrid R. (1967): "Legal education of the gentry at the inns of courts, 1560–1640." *Past and Present*, 38.

Prest, Wilfrid R. (1972): *The Inns of Courts under Elizabeth I and early Stuarts, 1590–1640*. London. Longman.

Prest, Wilfrid R. (2008): *William Blackstone: Law and letters in the eighteenth century*. Oxford. Oxford University Press.

Rademacher, Ludger (1999): "The Stanford Program for International Legal Studies (SPILS): An alternative to the 'classical' LlM program." *European Journal of Law Reform*, 1. no. 1–2.

Rama, Ángel (1984): *La ciudad letrada*. Hanover. Ediciones del Norte.

Ravelo, Ricardo (2006): *Los narcoabogados*. Mexico City. Grijalbo.

Reed, Alfred Z. (1921): *Training for the public profession of the law*. New York. Charles Scribner's Sons.

Reed, Alfred Z. (1928): *Present day law schools in the United States and Canada*. New York. Carnegie Foundation for the Advancement of Sciences.

Renoux-Zagamé, Marie F. (2007): "Domat, Jean." In P. Arabeyre, J. L. Halpérin, & J. Krynen, *Dictionnaire historique des juristes français, XIIᵉ–XXᵉ siècle*. Paris. Presses Universitaires de France.

Revista venezolana de legislación y jurisprudencia: Homenaje a los juristas españoles en Venezuela (2017): vol. 8.

Rheinstein, Max (1938): "Law faculties and law school: A comparison of legal education in the United States and Germany." *Wisconsin Law Review*.

Riesco, José A. (1976): "Conclusiones de la V conferencia de facultades y escuelas de derecho de América Latina: Informe del Relator General." In J. Witker, ed., *Antología de estudios sobre la enseñanza del derecho*. Mexico City. Universidad Nacional Autónoma de México.

Riggsby, Andrew M. (2010): *Roman law and the legal world of the Romans*. Cambridge. Cambridge University Press.

Rodrigues, Horácio W., & E. Junqueira (2002): *Ensino do direito no Brasil: Diretrizes curriculares e avaliação das condições de ensino*. Florianópolis. Fundação Boiteaux.

Rodríguez Cruz, Águeda M. (1973): *Historia de las universidades hispanoamericanas: Período hispánico*. Bogotá. Instituto Caro y Cuervo.

Roithmayr, Daria (1998): "Deconstructing the distinction between bias and merit." *La Raza Law Journal*, 10.

Roscio, Juan Germán (1817): *El triunfo de la libertad sobre el despotismo, en la confesión de un pensador arrepentido de sus errores políticos y dedicado a desagraviar la religión con el sistema de la tiranía*. Philadelphia. Imprenta de Thomas H. Palmer.

Rosenn, Keith (1969): "The reform of legal education in Brazil." *Journal of Legal Education*, 21.

Rotondi, Mario (1976): "Italia." In M. Rotondi, ed., *La science du droit au cours du dernier siècle*. Padua. CEDAM.

Sabsay, Fernando, & F. Barrancos y Vedia (1958): "La enseñanza del derecho." *Revista Jurídica de Buenos Aires*, 1.

Savatier, René (1976): "France." In M. Rotondi, ed., *La science du droit au cours du dernier siècle*. Padua. CEDAM.

Sbriccoli, Mario (1969): *L'interpretazione dello statuto: Contributo allo studio della funzione dei giuristi nell'età comunale*. Milan. A. Giuffré.

Schiavone, Aldo (2009): *Ius: La invención del derecho en Occidente*. Buenos Aires. Adriana Hidalgo Editora.

Schlegel, John H. (1985): "Between the Harvard founders and the American legal realists: The professionalization of the American law professor." *Journal of Legal Education*, 35.

Schulz, Fritz (1946): *History of Roman legal science*. Oxford. Clarendon Press.

Scotti, Luciana B. (2015): "Estanilao S. Zeballos: Maestro de la escuela argentina de derecho internacional privado en la Universidad de Buenos Aires." In T. Ortiz, ed., *Facultad de Derecho y Ciencias Sociales: Enseñanzas de su historia*. Buenos Aires. Universidad de Buenos Aires.

Serrano, Sol (1994): *Universidad y nación: Chile en el siglo XIX*. Santiago. Editorial Universitaria.

Serrano, Sol (2008): *¿Qué hacer con Dios en la República? Política y secularización en Chile (1845–1885)*. Mexico City. Fondo de Cultura Económica.

Silver, Carole (2013): "Holding onto 'too many lawyers': Bringing international graduate students to the front of the class." *Oñati Socio-Legal Series*, 3.

Squibb, George D. (1977): *Doctors' commons: A history of the college of advocates and doctors of law*. Oxford. Clarendon Press.

Stein, Peter (1992): "Roman law, common law, and civil law." *Tulane Law Review*, 66.

Stein, Peter (1999): *Roman law in European history*. Cambridge. Cambridge University Press.

Steiner, Henry (1971): "Legal education and socio-economic change: Brazilian perspectives." *American Journal of Comparative Law*, 19.

Stelling-Michaud, Sven (1955): *L'Université de Bologne et la pénétration des droits romain et canonique en Suisse aux XIIIe et XIVe siècles*. Geneva. Librairie E. Droz.

Stevens, Robert (1983): *Law school: Legal education in America from 1850s to the 1980s*. Chapel Hill. University of North Carolina Press.

Stoebuck, Willian B. (1968): "The reception of English common law in the American colonies." *William and Mary Law Review*, 10.

Sullivan, William M., et al. (2007): *Educating lawyers: Preparation for the profession of law*. San Francisco. John Wiley.

Summers, Robert S. (1984): *Lon F. Fuller*. London. Edward Arnold.

Sunkel, Osvaldo, & E. Fuenzalida (1979): "Transnational capitalism and national development." In J. J. Villamil, ed., *Transnational capitalism and national development*. Hassocks. Harvester Press.

Swaminathan, Shivaprasad (2019): "Mos geometricus and the common law mind: Interpreting contract theory." *Modern Law Review*, 82.

Tarello, Giovanni (1976): *Assolutismo e codificazione del diritto*. Bologna. Il Mulino.

Tarello, Giovanni (1988): *Cultura giuridica e politica del diritto*. Bologna. Il Mulino.

Tau Anzoátegui, Víctor (1987): *Las ideas jurídicas en Argentina*. Buenos Aires. Editorial Perrot.

Thireau, Jean-Louis (2007): "Pothier, Robert-Joseph." *Dictionnaire historique des juristes français: XIIᵉ-XXᵉ siècle*. Paris. Presses Universitaires de France.

Tocqueville, Alexis de (1990): *La démocratie en Amérique*. 1835–1840. Paris. J. Vrin.

Touraine, Alain (1974): *The academic system in American society*. New York. McGraw Hill.

Trazegnies, Fernando de (1979): *La idea de derecho en el Perú republican del siglo XIX*. Lima. Pontificia Universidad Católica del Perú.

Trubek, David, & M. Galanter (1974): "Scholars in Self-Estrangement: Some Reflections on the Crisis in Law and Development Studies in the United States" *Wisconsin Law Review*.

Tunc, André (1964): *Le droit des États-Unis*. Paris. Presses Universitaires de France.

Tünnermann Barheim, Carlos (1998): "La reforma universitaria de Córdoba." *Educación Superior y Sociedad*, 9, no. 1.

Turow, Scott (1977): *One L*. New York. Putnam.

Twining, William (1967): "Pericles and the plumber: Prolegomena to a working theory for lawyer education." *Law Quarterly Review*, 83.

Ugalde, Luis (1992): *El pensamiento teológico-político de Juan Germán Roscio*. Caracas. La Casa de Bello.

Unger, Roberto M. (1986): *The critical legal studies movement*. Cambridge. Harvard University Press.

Uribe-Urán, Víctor M. (2000): *Honorable lives: Lawyers, family and politics in Colombia 1780–1850*. Pittsburgh. University of Pittsburgh Press.

Valeur, Robert (1928): *L' enseignement du droit en France et aux États-Unis*. Paris. Marcel Giard.

Vides, M., M. Gómez, & L. F. Pérez-Hurtado (2011): "The American way: Los abogados latinoamericanos como estudiantes de maestría en Estados Unidos de América." *Boletín Mexicano de Derecho Comparado*, 130.

Verger, Jacques (1996): *La renaissance du XIIᵉᵐᵉ siècle*. Paris. Éditions du Cerf.

Villey, Michel (1962): *Leçons d'histoire de la philosophie du droit.* Paris. Dalloz.

Villey, Michel (1964): *Le droit romain.* 5th ed. Paris. Presses Universitaires de France.

Villey, Michel (1988): "La législation selon la Somme Théologique." In A. Giuliani and N. Picardi, eds., *Modelli di legislatore e scienza della legislazione.* Perugia. Edizione Scientifiche Italiane.

Walker, Clive (1993): "Legal education in England and Wales." *Oregon Law Review.*

Warren, Charles (1912): *A history of the American bar.* London. Cambridge University Press.

Wieacker, Franz (1980): *Storia del diritto privato moderno.* Milan. Giuffrè Editore.

Wilson, Richard (1989): "The new legal education in North and South America." *Stanford Journal of International Law,* 25.

Yanes, Francisco Javier (1959): *Idea general o principios elementales del derecho de gentes: Extractos de Vattel y otros autores.* 1824. Reproduced in Francisco Javier Yanes: *Manual político del venezolano.* Caracas. Academia Nacional de la Historia.

Zolezzi, Lorenzo (2017): *La enseñanza del derecho.* Lima. Pontificia Universidad Católica del Perú.

INDEX

academic freedom, 49

admission to law practice, 18; in ancient Rome, 13; in England, 58, 60, 62, 63–64; in Latin America, 39; in United States, 66, 69, 76

American Bar Association, 73, 75, 76

Ames, James, 72, 74

ancient Rome: classic period, 7, 9–12, 53; concept of law in, 5, 6, 9, 53; Justinian, 13–14, 53; postclassical period, 7, 12–14, 53; praetorian period, 7, 8–9; roots of European and Latin American law in, 5, 8

Antiquitatum romanorum jurisprudentiam ilustrantium syntagma (Heineccius), 26

Anti-Tribonianus (or *Hotomanus*; Hotman), 24

apprenticeship: in civil law tradition, 57; in classical Rome, 53; in common law tradition, 56–57; in England, 56, 58–60, 61, 62, 63; in English colonies, 65; in Latin America, 39, 52; in Middle Ages, 23; in United States, 65, 66, 67, 69–70

Argentina, 48–50

barristers, 58–62

Bello, Andrés, 44, 45; *Principios de derecho de gentes (Principles of International Law)*, 45

Bentham, Jeremy, 42, 43, 46

Blackstone, William, 62–63, 66, 69, 109n5; *Commentaries on the Laws of England*, 62

Bologna Declaration of 1999, 99

Bracton (or *De legibus et consuetudinibus Angliae; The laws and customs of England*), 59, 61

Brandeis, Louis, 78

Brazil: Colonial education, 35; Dantas lecture, 90, 94; establishment of law schools, 42; law school

The authorized representative in the EU for product safety and compliance is:
Mare Nostrum Group
B.V Doelen 72
4831 GR Breda
The Netherlands

www.ingramcontent.com/pod-product-compliance
Lightning Source LLC
Chambersburg PA
CBHW021815190326
41518CB00007B/605